To order additional copies of *Authentic,* by Scott R. Ward,
call **1-800-765-6955.**
Visit us at **www.reviewandherald.com** for information
on other Review and Herald® products.

AUTHENTIC

Where true, life-changing Christianity begins}

SCOTT R. WARD

REVIEW AND HERALD® PUBLISHING ASSOCIATION

Since 1861 | www.reviewandherald.com

Published by Review and Herald® Publishing Association, Hagerstown, MD 21741-1119

Review and Herald® titles may be purchased in bulk for educational, business, fund-raising, or sales promotional use. For information, e-mail SpecialMarkets@reviewandherald.com.

The Review and Herald® Publishing Association publishes biblically based materials for spiritual, physical, and mental growth and Christian discipleship.

The author assumes full responsibility for the accuracy of all facts and quotations as cited in this book.

Unless otherwise indicated, Scripture quotations are taken from the *Holy Bible,* New Living Translation, copyright © 1996, 2004, 2007 by Tyndale House Foundation. Used by permission of Tyndale House Publishers, Inc., Carol Stream, Illinois 60188. All rights reserved.

Bible texts marked KJV are from the King James Version.

Texts credited to NKJV are from the New King James Version. Copyright © 1979, 1980, 1982 by Thomas Nelson, Inc. Used by permission. All rights reserved.

This book was
Edited by Gerald Wheeler
Copyedited by Jeremy J. Johnson
Interior designed by Emily Ford / Review and Herald® Design Center
Cover designed by Joe La Com
Cover photo by Aimee Burchard
Typeset: Minion Pro 11/13

PRINTED IN U.S.A.

16 15 14 13 12   5 4 3 2 1

Library of Congress Cataloging-in-Publication Data
Ward, Scott R.
  Authentic : committed for life / Scott R. Ward.
     p. cm.
  1. Spiritual life—Christianity. 2. Bible. N.T. Gospels--Criticism, interpretation, etc. 3. Great Commission (Bible) I. Title.
  BV4501.3.W3617 2012
  248.4—dc23
                              2012016005

ISBN 978-0-8280-2632-1

Dedication
To my children Paige, Erin, and Hunter.

My prayer for you is that you will find intimacy
with Jesus at a much younger age than I did.

Acknowledgments

Thanks to Alan Walshe, my D.Min. major professor and advisor, for encouraging me to join the cohort in discipleship and biblical spirituality at the Theological Seminary at Andrews University. This book is a direct result of my research as I taught and studied spiritual growth in my on-campus Christian clubs at both Adventist and public high schools.

Special thanks to Jon Dybdahl for reading along and encouraging me chapter by chapter as I wrote my thoughts and experiences down, and especially for challenging me to include a practical application section that became Part V.

Thanks also to the others who took the time to read and offer suggestions and encouragement as I worked on this project: Tina de Sousa, Lana Brauer, Roy Ice, Brian and Siran Lenser, Del Dunavant, Josh Tenborg, and Bart Vogel, just to name a few.

I would also like to thank John McCann for being a spiritual friend and tremendous supporter both personally and in my ministry.

And, of course, praise and thanksgiving to my Jesus for drawing near and guiding me into this life and journey that will last for all of eternity, and then some.

HIGH SCHOOL OUTREACH

www.livingiths.org

Contents

Part IV: Experiencing His Power

The Gospel Commission According to Mark: Miracles, Signs, and Wonders

Part V: Living Life Devotionally

Taking Action: Establishing Your Own Testimony

Introduction

Personal Spirituality and the Fourfold Gospel Commission

God has created you for a very special reason. Would you like to find out what it is? The Lord has an incredibly rewarding future for you. Would you like to know how to pursue it? God created you because He wants to know you personally and spend time with you and care for you like the very special son or daughter that He has meant you to be. Then within that special relationship Jesus wants to spend time with you engaging in "the mission" together—giving purpose and meaning to your life.

The Christian "mission" is the gospel commission. But we can't effectively take the gospel into all the world until we start grasping its meaning for ourselves by experiencing it in our lives. So we will look at the gospel commission in the context of our personal relationships with Jesus. He invites us all to join Him in fulfilling the great gospel commission, because it is the mission itself that helps to develop our characters and all the various relationships—with God and with others—that will be ours for eternity.

Since God intended the Christian life to be saturated with mission, we will be taking an in-depth look at the gospel commission as recorded by all four Gospel writers. They interpret or reinterpret historical events from a variety of viewpoints, and the gospel commission is no exception. The more viewpoints we consider, the more accurate view we have of what Jesus really said on the Mount of Olives on that day.

We will first look at the Gospel of John, in which Jesus gave the commission on an intimate and personal level to Peter. Three times Jesus asked him, "Do you love Me?" And three times the disciple answered, "Yes, Lord, You know that I love You" (see John 21:15-17). The commissioning here is based on a love relationship with Jesus, and the commission is stated as "*Go,* feed My sheep." The love relationship with Jesus seen here and throughout Peter's life is the foundation of the overall commission that we are each to take on personally as well.

Next we will look at the commission according to Luke. Luke's emphasis is to wait for the promised filling of the Holy Spirit before *going*. Without the Holy Spirit in our lives, we face the danger of sliding into legalistic teeth-gritting effort. But when we are filled with the Spirit of God rather than the spirit of self, the world can be turned upside down, and thousands can be converted in a day!

After Luke we will examine Matthew's version, with its emphasis not only on teaching but on discipling as well. This last part often gets left out. But without genuinely caring for people in discipling relationships, they will not be able to understand that Jesus loves them and wants a relationship with them in a personal way too. We are the hands, feet, and face of Jesus' love to the world.

Then we will turn to the Gospel of Mark. It indicates that the true commission being carried out will manifest itself not only by "disciple making" but through "miracle working" as well. When God's power is truly unleashed wonders will abound. And wonders do abound right now as we speak. Miracles take place in God's name the world over.

Finally, we will consider some practical ways to organize your personal devotional life so that you can actually live out the life that Jesus wants for each of us to enjoy here on earth. We will examine everything from how to structure effectively your personal daily devotions to making sure that you plan such great spiritual adventures as Bible conferences and camp meetings as part of your personal spiritual life every year.

So settle in and pray for the Spirit of God to guide you through this journey that is saturated with Scripture and common sense. Then, as you read, plead for God to convict you of what He would have you to *do* with what you learn, because this is where the true life-changing Christianity that you've heard about in stories begins!

"Christ's method alone will give true success in reaching the people. The Savior mingled with men as one who desired their good. He showed His sympathy for them, ministered to their needs, and won their confidence. Then He bade them, 'Follow Me'" (*The Ministry of Healing,* p. 143).

Part I

Knowing Him Personally

The Gospel Commission According to John: The Call of Love

"After breakfast Jesus asked Simon Peter, 'Simon son of John, do you love me more than these?'

"'Yes, Lord,' Peter replied, 'you know I love you.'

"'Then feed my lambs,' Jesus told him.

"Jesus repeated the question: 'Simon son of John, do you love me?'

"'Yes, Lord,' Peter said, 'you know I love you.'

"'Then take care of my sheep,' Jesus said.

"A third time he asked him, 'Simon son of John, do you love me?'

"Peter was hurt that Jesus asked the question a third time. He said, 'Lord, you know everything. You know that I love you.'

"Jesus said, 'Then feed my sheep'" (John 21:15-17).

The gospel commission according to John emphasizes being filled with love for Jesus so as to make your life and mission on earth happy and successful. Just as with Peter, it doesn't matter how many times we fail—Jesus is always there to pick us up and give us another chance, because He desperately wants to be a part of our lives now and throughout all eternity. And our relationship with Him not only makes Him happy, but is also the healthiest way for us to live. Only when we know Jesus personally and intimately can His love fill us and help us to be the best and happiest that we can be. It is only in relationship that we begin fully to feel and experience Jesus' grace in our lives.

Chapter 1

The Mystery of Love—
What Is It, Anyway?

Jesus Loves Me" may be the best-known Christian song of all time. While children know it, many—perhaps most—adults have never experienced it in a practical way. How do you feel loved by a God that you cannot see, touch, hear, or smell in the normal way? I'm going to go out on a limb here and state that in my opinion most adults have never felt genuinely loved by God. In fact, I'm not even sure that we know what love is. I'm still trying to figure it out myself.

Most Christians at some time in their lives have said "Jesus loves you" to someone. And yet Jesus' love is a foreign concept to most people. At least the evidence found in statistical studies reveals the fact that most Christians today do *not* live a lifestyle much different than their non-Christian counterparts. Studies by the Barna Group reveal that there is statistically almost no difference between Christians and non-Christians when it comes to engaging in such activities as lying, pornography, and divorce. Isn't love supposed to be life-changing—especially God's love? The behavior of such so-called Christians (that's you and me) suggests that God's love is not being experienced as a practical life-changing reality on a day-to-day basis. Maybe it's because the concept of love in general has become rather confused.

Almost everyone in America has said the words "I love _____." Often the expression involves chocolate or some kind of entertainment, yet a great number of such individuals have also expressed love for a person— at least meaning that they "love" what that person can do for them or that the individual makes them feel good in some way. And easily the most frequent misapplication of the word love is when it's applied to gratuitous uncommitted sex—thank you, Hollywood! We all want it to be like it is in the movies and beer commercials—right? Obviously we've been told lies about love, and we've believed them.

To get a fuller understanding of Jesus' love and the "commission to love" that He gave to Peter in John 21, we need to start by going back to the beginning of the Bible and take a look at God's desire for a people to love as His very own children. This will help us to understand more about God's great rescue effort that He challenged Peter to engage in. And the story goes like this . . .

Created for Relationships: We Are God's Family

In the beginning God was lonely. But how could that be? After all, He had thousands of angels surrounding Him, and in addition to them the author of Hebrews refers to other "worlds" (Heb. 1:2, KJV; 11:3, KJV), implying that God has created other kinds of "beings" somewhere out there to interact with as well. Job 2:1 also talks about the "sons of God" (KJV) coming to present themselves before the Lord, Satan being among them. Satan was then representing Planet Earth—which leads us to assume that the others were also delegates for other places too. And yet in Genesis 1:26 God said: "Let us make human beings in our image, to be like us." So even though other creatures did exist, none of them bore God's image specifically, and it seems that He wanted beings more like Himself. Ezekiel 1 has an amazing description of angels. The rather bizarre language it uses suggests that they are far beyond what human words and concepts can grasp, as we will discuss later. But for now, one thing is for sure: angels don't naturally look the way they do when they take on human form and appear to people here on earth! They are amazingly complex and intricate according to Ezekiel's depiction—but somehow not fully bearing God's image.

So being created in God's image was something new and revolutionary. When Ellen White comments on what it means to be made in God's image, she says: "Man was to bear God's image, both in outward resemblance and in character" (*Patriarchs and Prophets,* p. 45). God's character is one of love. Thus when we act in loving ways, we do so consistently with His character (also revealed by God's law). Scripture sums up the law as: "'Love the Lord your God with all your heart, with all your soul, with all your strength, and with all your mind,' and 'your neighbor as yourself'" (Luke 10:27, NKJV). The Bible intentionally states the law in relational terms, that is, how people are to interact with each other and with God. Love is the highest goal in all that we do. This is what it means to have God's character—to be loving and kind to all creatures, people, and God. Because love and kindness inherently involves very personal actions, it cannot be cold, indifferent, or aloof—it is warm and intimate.

We don't know what the characters of God's other creatures are like, but we do know how He created us to be. And we also know that the creation of humans was so special and unique that it very likely contributed to Satan's jealousy. We have no scriptural record of Satan tempting beings other than the angels and humans. After God expelled Satan from heaven, He allowed him to present his "alternative" lifestyle to Adam and Eve after the Lord completed creation. Thus Satan sets the example of how *not* to be loving, and God through Jesus sets the example of how *to* be loving. Thus we have good pitted against evil—all couched in the relational terms of whom we will choose to follow, listen to, and spend time with.

We find evidence of God's close personal relationship with people in Genesis 3:8, in which we read: "When the cool evening breezes were blowing, the man and his wife heard the Lord God walking about in the garden." It is direct proof that God Himself came regularly to walk and talk with the people whom He had created—they recognized the sound of His approach. Scripture offers no indication that humans were an experiment, or pets, or merely created to be subjects. In fact, John 15:15 declares: "I no longer call you slaves, because a master doesn't confide in his slaves. Now you are my friends, since I have told you everything the Father told me." The Gospels show a clear record that Jesus came to earth to be with, laugh with, love, and care for His children that He had created so many years before. He longed to walk with His people again and to try to convince them to choose to live with Him for eternity. Jesus healed, taught, and mentored them tirelessly up until His dying breath on the cross. Even with death at the door He thought not of Himself but of His people. Hanging on the cross, He forgave the soldiers gambling for His possessions, asked John to care for His mother, and promised the repentant thief next to Him eternal life. A few hours earlier He had lovingly given a look of forgiveness to Peter after his prophesied denial. This one act of forgiveness changed the disciple's life forever and paved the way for Jesus to commission him to go to all the world "feeding sheep" out of love for his master. Such examples are just a fraction of the myriad personal interactions between God and His people depicted throughout Scripture. God's recorded history with His people is a very personal and relational one. And He not only wanted to come and be with us and know us, but He longs for us to know Him as well.

God revealed Himself personally to all humanity—not just to those present during Jesus' incarnation. For that reason He gave us His written Word to recount His time on earth. It also details many of His other interactions with people through divine providence and miracles—and He communicated all of it in a way that we as humans could understand. The Lord didn't drop a book from the sky with interesting tales of His life in heaven with angels in order to help us learn more about Him. Instead, He miraculously spoke to prophets who were dedicated to Him and were engaged in committed relationships with Him, and He did so in terms that they could understand and relate to. He used practical illustrations from everyday occurrences so that we could know Him and love Him in the best and most personal way possible.

The obvious lesson here is that God created us to be relational beings—it is both our nature and that of God Himself. He made us in His image, and we relate best to each other when we are reflecting His own character of love. God speaks to us and interacts with us through our relational everyday patterns and rhythms because it is our nature, and we cannot communicate in any other way.

We exist because of a loving God that created us for relationships with Him—we are His family. John 1 reveals that Jesus Himself formed Adam with His own hands and stooped over to breathe into his nostrils His own breath of life. And it was the same Jesus who was sitting there asking Peter if he loved Him. I wonder how fully the disciple grasped the fact that it was indeed the Creator of the universe he was talking to. How much did he understand of what it meant to tell his God that he loved Him with every fiber of his being? Does Jesus still think back to that moment with misty eyes as He remembers the incredible conversion that happened in Peter's life and how the disciple went on to serve Him so passionately and so well? And I also wonder if Jesus sees a little of Peter in each of us today. Furthermore, how many of us realize that Jesus is looking at each one of us with forgiveness and love, just as He did Peter?

Now Do You Know What Love Is?

So what kind of definition can we put to the word "love"? I still don't think I have a very good understanding of what love is—only what love does. God's love obviously comes packed with action! Just look at 1 Corinthians 13—the famous love chapter. It's not a definition of love—it's a description of what love does. But modern love isn't always like this, is it? I think that's a huge part of the problem—it's mostly hollow statements and unbacked currency. Love isn't a state of being but a state of action. The words "I love you" can never stand alone. Even though you claim to love someone, if you don't reflect it in your behavior, how much does it really mean?

So you say you're a Christian and you love Jesus. How much time have you spent with Him lately and how meaningful was it? Have you gone out and done anything with Him lately? You've read the Gospels—you know what He likes to do. If you wish your relationship with your Creator was more meaningful and more active—keep reading. We're going to take a look at David's love for God that involved lots of action but went way deeper than that. His deeds were rooted in something far deeper than a legalistic feeling of obligation. In Psalm 63 he pours out his heart in incredibly emotion-charged language that reveals a loving attachment to his God rarely seen in our world today. So let's get a little sentimental here and see how it helps us to connect with our God.

"The more closely believers have walked with God, the more clearly and powerfully have they testified of their Redeemer's love and of His saving grace" (*The Acts of the Apostles,* p. 49).

Chapter 2

Nurturing the Relationship

"O God, you are my God;
I earnestly search for you.
My soul thirsts for you;
my whole body longs for you
in this parched and weary land
where there is no water.
I have seen you in your sanctuary
and gazed upon your power and glory.
Your unfailing love is better than life itself;
how I praise you!
I will praise you as long as I live,
lifting up my hands to you in prayer.
You satisfy me more than the richest feast.
I will praise you with songs of joy.
I lie awake thinking of you,
meditating on you through the night.
Because you are my helper,
I sing for joy in the shadow of your wings.
I cling to you;
your strong right hand holds me securely."
—Ps. 63:1-8

But First—Memory Lane . . .

When I was a kid, I loved Christmastime at Grandma's house. The fragrance of the fresh-cut evergreen from Grandpa's back 40, the dancing and flickering light from the fireplace, and the loving care baked into the taste of Grandma's cinnamon apple pie. Mashed potatoes with egg gravy and stuffing, Christmas carols sung with family and friends, a warm embrace, and mistletoe, of course! We enjoyed the world's thickest fudge with walnuts galore, crispy caramel popcorn to share, and cousins telling the cleanest, funniest jokes you'd ever heard. Secret recipe homemade ice cream with more than a dozen table games to play till way past bedtime, and brightly colorful packages and gifts all around. Those are some of the fondest memories from my childhood Christmases at Grandpa and Grandma's house. Although surrounded by the ice and snow of the central Minnesota winter on the outside, it was filled with the glow of visiting aunts, uncles, cousins, and friends on the inside. It was one of our family traditions that no one ever wanted to miss. I cherish those memories, and I miss those times still today.

When I read Psalm 63, the warmth and intimacy of David's relationship with God reminds me of my childhood family ties like the Christmas ones I've described above. It's so sad that most Christians fail to connect with Jesus in the same multisensory way that we do with loved ones during the holidays. What if we could somehow learn to transfer some of the same complexity and fervor of the human relationships we experienced during such special times to our daily encounters with Jesus throughout the year? What if we could figure out how to develop healthy family-style love with Him?

I've tried to remember the things that I used to do to show my grandparents that I loved them back after all the things they'd done for me. Review your own relationships—the healthy ones, that is. What is it that makes people feel loved in return? What's the key?

Human love at its best within marriage (as God created it in the beginning) is multisensory, complex, and secure. If it consisted only of speaking and listening, the institution would never survive. (I'm employing the married relationships here because Jesus describes us as His bride and uses marriage metaphors for His relationship with us throughout Scripture.)

And yet somehow, after investing so much into the complexity of human relationships, including special celebrations such as Christmas, we think that a mere one-page devotional in the morning followed by a quick prayer on the way out the door should be enough to keep us close to God. But then we are confused when we feel distant from Him and lack the strength and peace that we need to get through life. And we accuse *Him* of being distant and uncaring—the nerve!

Think about the time you spend with Jesus every day—would that same amount of time and effort produce an award-winning marriage? Would it be enough to keep your children close and help them to know how to live their lives to the fullest? Let's take a look at David's love for, and time with, Jesus in Psalm 63 to get some ideas on how to improve. We will discuss the first, most emotional part here and then look at the rest of the passage in the next chapter.

David's Passion for God

"O God, you are my God" (verse 1). Here we have a powerful personal statement of a felt fact—a fact based on an emotion so strong that it has become a reality in David's life. Not an entry-level beginning relationship with God, it is rather one of comfort and security! The psalm is far beyond the basics of relationship, and obviously it is Spirit-filled and confident. David had publicly committed his life to God and had been living life with Him for many years. The Lord had used him in obvious ways again and again. Now, as he ran for his life from King Saul, he fearlessly poured out his heart to God, showing confidence in and dedication to his maker and friend.

That is what a real relationship with God feels like. And I say "feels" intentionally, because it is a very emotional psalm. The description of their relationship here is not based on facts and understandings but more on intuition, revealing how closely he is attached to his God—it's personal.

"I earnestly search for you" (verse 1). We could also describe it as to seek passionately. Passion is with the heart more than with the mind. Obviously our relationships with God have rational elements in understanding teachings about Him and in intentionally engaging the relationship. But the intense personal emotional attachment brought on by the Spirit of the living God is what fuels the desire and need to cling to Him through the ups and downs of life. Furthermore, it is what inspires us to reach out and offer to others the same lifesaving relationship that we've found for ourselves. It is the driving force in David's life.

"My soul thirsts for you" (verse 1). How does a soul thirst? Once again, we encounter a largely unexplainable emotion. A metaphor for an unquenchable desire for God, it seeks to depict the innate longing for Himself that our Maker has placed inside each of us. Not only has David identified it—he has even nurtured it into a full-blown passion. Most people don't even recognize that this innate hunger for fulfillment comes from God.

People mistakenly try to satisfy their desire for God with worldly possessions and passions. When the Lord called me out of the world, He led me to read about this concept in the preface to *The Desire of Ages* and to realize that all I had been searching for could only be found in Him. The worldly college party scene seemed fun at first, but it didn't satisfy my desires long-term—rather it intensified my sense of guilt and shame and left me emptier than before. The thirst of the soul can only be truly quenched by connecting with the living God of heaven and earth and allowing Him to fill and fulfill us. All other attempts to meet the desire will eventually leave us eaten away and hurting on the inside—spiritually emaciated.

"My whole body longs for you in this parched and weary land where there is no water" (verse 1). Truly there is no living water in this world as we know it. One day when our Savior re-creates our planet such water will once again give life as in the Garden of Eden, but until then our world is a mere shell of what it used to be. Here David expands the metaphor from the thirst of the soul to the longing of the body as well by stating that the thirst is so powerful that his entire body has dried up just as the landscape around him is.

Perhaps David wrote his psalm near the end of the dry season when Israel had gone months without rain. The central valley in California where I live has a similar climate. When we go hiking in the mountains in August, near the end of our dry season, the trails have become fine powdery dust that covers everything. The only way the majestic oak trees survive those long periods of drought is through the deep root systems they have established to tap the moisture left in the ground from the rainy months of the year.

In the same way, David's years of love and devotion to God while watching sheep as a youth grew the deep roots that sustained him during the years of hardship and drought that only God knew were ahead. Helping our children and youth develop their relationships with God early on, and showing them how to tap into His love, are foundational tasks that every parent, church, and Christian school must take to heart. We know that all our children will eventually face trials and hard times, and if they have no depth with God, they will be vulnerable and eventually succumb to the lure of the world.

I desperately wish to foster this educated hunger for God to the point that crying out to Jesus has become my second nature and reaction to anything that life throws my way. If the president of your country were hunting you down like an animal as David's king did him, what would you do? Would your first, deepest, and most constant thoughts be of God as David's were? May God help us all to reach that point.

Chapter 3

Multisensory Relationships and Worship

"I have seen you in your sanctuary
and gazed upon your power and glory."
—Ps. 63:2

Many evangelical Christians don't have a good understanding of what the Old Testament sanctuary is all about. As a youth pastor I run Christian clubs at public and private high schools in the town where I live. In the Adventist school when I start to talk about the sanctuary the kids whine that it's so boring—they've heard the dry facts and theological disputes all their lives. But at my public school Christian club that young people from many denominations attend, most give me a blank stare when I ask if they know what it was. Out of 40 or more kids only the twin sons of a pastor have heard of it. Many of the others say that they read only the New Testament. But whether you've been bored to death about the sanctuary or know little or nothing about it, I believe you have an amazing treat in store in the next few pages.

OK—rewind back to my grandma's house. That's how the sanctuary depicts God's "house." You don't understand? Yes, devotionally the sanctuary was a multisensory worship experience. I imagine that every time David made the pilgrimage there to worship his God his mind would flash back to sanctuary visits as a child. His thoughts would fill with loving memories of aunts, uncles, cousins, and friends all coming to worship together for extended periods of time.

Then, as David approached even closer, the visual must have combined with the first faint hints of the smell of barbecue for an even greater impact. Yes, barbecue! Even though I've been a vegetarian for many years, I still love the aroma of meat cooking on a grill. And in the courtyard of the sanctuary the first thing you came to was the altar of burnt offering.

There the priests would cut up the sacrificial animals and present them to the Lord, symbolizing the Lamb of God, who would be slain for the world—Jesus' crucifixion. The meat was not all burnt to a crisp, either. Much of it would be food for the priests and their families, and so the aroma of the barbecue was called a sweet-smelling sacrifice to the Lord (see Ex. 29:18, 25, and countless other passages, sometimes translated as "pleasing aroma").

As a vegetarian and dessert lover I still prefer the smell of Grandma's apple pie—but you get the point. They would have been wonderful memories for David of his family and his God. Then as the king came even closer to the sanctuary the smell of the incense burning inside the first compartment must have permeated the air as well. I imagine that for him and for other Israelites the scent of the incense not only reminded them of the priest's prayers ascending to heaven, but that it represented their own personal connection with God as well. I would think that at this point the presence of the Lord could be felt too—because He was right there! The incense in the first compartment would waft up and over the curtain and into the Most Holy Place, which housed the ark of the covenant. The ark contained the mercy seat, which is where God's very presence rested and remained in Israel's midst.

Remember the old movie *Raiders of the Lost Ark* with a young Harrison Ford? It's not totally accurate in its depiction of the ark, but one thing was clear—the ark housed otherworldly power! In the real ark God's presence was actually there. Jewish legend has it that during the more corrupt times in Israel's history when people bought and sold the office of the high priest, the other priests would tie a rope around the ankle of the high priest so that if he went into the Most Holy Place before God in an inappropriate manner and the presence of the Lord struck him dead, they could drag his body out. No kidding—God was really there, and He was holy and He still is holy, and sin can't survive directly in His presence.

And yet if you loved God as David did, you had nothing to be afraid of—there was only pure joy in His presence! In fact, David was so comfortable with the Lord that one time when he was fleeing from King Saul he went to the sanctuary and ate some of the bread from the table of showbread, something that he wasn't supposed to do. It wasn't for nonpriests—not even for those anointed to be king. But God overlooked David's desperate physical hunger, because he consistently satisfied his spiritual hunger with Him at the sanctuary as well. David was the only person in all of

Scripture known as a man after God's own heart. I would give anything to have a heart like that!

As I recently rediscovered the sanctuary and its multisensory ministry, I wondered how that aspect of its meaning got lost. I've heard about the sanctuary all my life—but never like this. Since then I've fallen in love with the richness of what was only theology to me before.

The wrap-up—or the payoff, if you will—appears in the next few verses of Psalm 63:

> "O God, you are my God;
> I earnestly search for you.
> My soul thirsts for you;
> my whole body longs for you
> in this parched and weary land
> where there is no water.
> I have seen you in your sanctuary
> and gazed upon your power and glory.
> Your unfailing love is better than life itself;
> how I praise you!
> I will praise you as long as I live,
> lifting up my hands to you in prayer.
> You satisfy me more than the richest feast.
> I will praise you with songs of joy.
> I lie awake thinking of you,
> meditating on you through the night.
> Because you are my helper,
> I sing for joy in the shadow of your wings.
> I cling to you;
> your strong right hand holds me securely."
> —Ps. 63:1-8

Do you see the results of the relationship? Can you imagine yourself feeling that God's "unfailing love is better than life itself" (verse 3)? Do you remember Paul saying that although he would rather die and wait for the Lord, it was more beneficial for him to stay and help people on earth? He felt what David did too. Both knew what Enoch experienced. The way they are talking sounds as if they would rather walk to God's house, as Enoch did, and just live with Him than stay in our sin-sick world. Oh, just to leave the troubles of our world and begin an eternity of peace and happiness with Jesus in the new earth right now—what a dream! And to express that joy, David spends the next couple verses breaking into praise! He can't help himself. Psalm 150 goes even further and urges us to praise God in His sanctuary with horns and lyres and harps and with the tambourine and dance and stringed instruments and flutes. The psalmist even goes on to tell us to praise Him with loud clashing cymbals!

Many of the churches I've attended find flutes and harps acceptable, but don't you dare bring in the loud crashing cymbals and tambourines—unless, of course, it's the academy concert band performing. And dance? Let's not even go there! But wait—what's wrong with this picture? Why are we so pent up and tense when we praise God? I still like organ music and some praise bands—but I'm not ready to dance before the Lord. Do you think that says something about my relationship with Jesus?

Finally, in Psalm 63:6 you can just see the love in David's eyes even though they're closed, can't you? Lying on his bed "meditating" on God throughout the night! Really? Who today does that except for those newly fallen in love as they think about their significant other? This psalm is so incredible in its passion and intensity. I wish I felt that way. I'm trying to—I want it more than anything. Don't you?

"It would be well to spend a thoughtful hour each day reviewing the life of Christ from the manger to Calvary. We should take it point by point and let the imagination vividly grasp each scene, especially the closing ones of His earthly life. By thus contemplating His teachings and sufferings, and the infinite sacrifice made by Him for the redemption of the race, we may strengthen our faith, quicken our love, and become more deeply imbued with the spirit which sustained our Savior" (*Maranatha*, p. 77).

Chapter 4

Multisensory Devotional Practices

We as Christians need to do a better job of getting past the details of the individual words of the Bible and discover their meaning as a whole. I believe that Jesus wants us actually to live them out. The Bible is richer and deeper and far more miraculous than we give it credit for. It is a living book. While we already do know the reality of the living Word in some ways, we just need to focus on doing it more often.

During Communion we experience the textures of the bread and juice in our mouths and the taste and smell of them as well. The warm water pouring over our feet and the tickle of the cotton towel that dries them during the foot-washing ceremony reminds us of our baptisms, during which we felt our bodies being immersed under the water, then being symbolically resurrected to new life in Jesus as the water swirled around us, while at the same moment hearing the amens of the congregation as we emerge victorious in Jesus.

Since during such special services we use all five senses, why not engage more of them on a daily basis in our devotions to make our relationships with Jesus more intense and meaningful and intimate too? So let's try to take some of David's experiences in the sanctuary and apply them to our own devotional lives today.

Daily Applications for Us . . .

When I first started thinking about how David must have experienced the sanctuary, I was jealous. I wanted to experience those ancient traditions and symbols as well—to see and smell and feel God's presence in as many tangible ways as possible. Thus I started bringing sanctuary symbols into my devotional time in the best way that I could think of, and it amazed me how God still responds to our efforts to sense His presence.

At the time I had been enjoying a rich devotional time that revolved around praying scriptures that I had memorized as a child. As I prayed such passages five days a week for several years I slowly discovered ever greater depths of their meaning. But gradually I started feeling a need for a change in my devotional routine. No matter how well my devotions may be going, God always seems to make me change every so often, and rediscovering the sanctuary was exactly what I needed at that time.

It was into this rich scripture-filled setting and experience that I brought a small incense burner, because I wanted to know why God had made that such an integral part of the Old Testament sanctuary. I had ordered the incense burner online along with several kinds of incense, including frankincense and myrrh, two of the gifts for Baby Jesus from the Wise Men. It was with great anticipation that I tore open the boxes when they finally arrived. That first morning as I lit the incense and sat back to spend time with God, I was just amazed at my reaction.

I felt both peaceful and intrigued at the same time. The scent brought back memories of Christmas pageants from years gone by, just as I'm sure it reminded David of former visits with family to the sanctuary. It also reminded me that my mother had lit incense in our home on Friday nights when I was a child. It focused my mind on God and the things of God in a new and deeper way. As I just watched the smoke ascend in swirling patterns into the room while the fragrance filled the place, I thought about frankincense and myrrh in ways that I had never done before. For example, I wondered what they must have meant to Jesus' family and later to Him when He was told the story for the first time as a boy. Why had the Wise Men brought those gifts, and what was their significance? What had made them so valuable then, and what was their value today in a spiritual sense?

Several days later my candelabra came in the mail, and I eagerly set it up along with the incense. It was a dark and dreary day outside, so the window light was particularly dim, allowing the candlelight to glow especially bright. I was absolutely captivated by what it must have been like to be a priest ministering before God in the sanctuary and witnessing the light of the real candelabra piercing the darkness of the first compartment of the sanctuary. It now reminds me on a daily basis that God wants to be the light of the world through me—through my hands and feet and voice, and through the love that a relationship with Him brings into my heart.

Such sanctuary symbols help me to focus during my devotional time, but I don't use them every day. Sometimes I might play some Christian music that may remind me of what the Temple choir may have sounded like. Other days I just might sit back and enjoy the stillness of silence. I have personally found that adding the senses of sight and smell and sound to my devotions, just as Jesus had instructed the Jews to do so long ago, adds a depth to my devotions that is life-changing indeed.

I still haven't figured out a way to create a meaningful devotional cracker to represent the bread of the presence, but I have found that a variety of herbal teas or other hot drinks can add the depth of the sense of taste to my experience as well. They are just multisensory things that remind me of Jesus and time spent with Him just as the sights, sounds, smells, and tastes of Christmas remind me of my family gatherings as a child. The sights, sounds, smells, and tastes of the sanctuary surely affected its participants as well—just as God intended them to.

I'm sure that not everybody will embrace such symbols, because we all have different personality types, but the point is to try to experience God through more than just seeing and feeling the printed pages of the Bible. Experiment by adding new elements to your devotional times and see what happens. Even as I use various symbols at different times they still lead up to and involve prayer and devotional Bible reading, yet they add a depth and a focus that I've never experienced before. And remember, God established them for all His people thousands of years ago.

Although since the cross Old Testament ceremonial law no longer requires us to use such sanctuary symbols, many people still find them devotionally significant today. And even though hippies in the 1960s and 1970s burned incense and New Age movements employ candles, that doesn't mean they are inappropriate—such symbols belonged to God first. While other groups may have hijacked or misused them, we should not take them away from God's people, who had them originally.

Many of my students and members of my church now replace the ancient candelabra and incense with scented candles during their devotional times as they pray and read scriptures. It serves the same devotional purpose for them and is more convenient in many ways. The point is to pursue communion with God and Jesus in any way that you can, to try everything you know in an effort to experience Him in the most powerful ways possible in your life today. The result will be a greater sense of peace in this life and an incredible eternity with our Savior in heaven and the new earth.

Now let's move beyond our daily devotional practices and look at other semiregular activities that you can use to deepen your relationship with God.

Chapter 5

More Ways to Strengthen Your Love for Jesus

Several years ago I heard about a person whose devotional routine included spending a half day per month in prayer. I love going out into nature so that I can get away from the distractions of life and thus concentrate on God just as Jesus did in Gethsemane. Such things rarely seem to happen on their own, so I decided to add this one to my own regular schedule. It has turned out to be a great time to refocus my life. I don't always make it every month, but when I do it is extremely refreshing! So much of life involves just making yourself do things, isn't it? That's the bottom line for most of the things presented in this book—are you just going to talk about it, or will you actually do it? Here is an excerpt from my journal on one of my half days of prayer:

"Today is my half day of prayer, and I brought my computer with me so that I could journal my experience to share with you. I typically come to a large park just outside of the town where I live. There are 100 acres or more of park, a zoo, and a golf course. I have fond, fun, social memories of the golf course—even though I'm not a good golfer and rarely get to play. And I've taken my kids to the little zoo a few times too—it's a good clean family place. Anyway, on my prayer days I head straight for the Japanese garden, and I walk around some and then sit on the porch of a Japanese style teahouse that's located in the middle of the garden.

"As I walked up to the teahouse today my thoughts were different than ever before because of all the things I've been experiencing with multisensory spirituality. When I write, it's about fresh and new things—not things I've been doing for years—so I'm sharing my own journey with you here as I experience it.

"So as I walked up through the main park I thought about all the families that go here on the weekends to have picnics and barbecues, and guess what popped into my mind? The altar of burnt offering! And it made me smile and reminded me to pray. I'm sure that must sound really weird to most of you, but that is my goal—sensory connectors that remind me of God wherever I go. As I rounded the corner into the garden and headed toward the porch where I sit, I instantly noticed that someone had left the outdoor courtyard lights on. Just now as I began typing I turned and glanced at them again and remembered the candelabra and that God wants me to be the light of the world. I wonder if He planned all this to happen today?

"Anyway, it is overcast and cool. My iPhone says 54 degrees and 92 percent humidity. That strikes me as being rather postmodern—being in nature and thinking of God with a laptop and smartphone. We live in a complex and contradictory world, don't we? Now as I'm ready to focus, a train comes rumbling past and reminds me that the world is a very distracting place and that finding true peace and time with God is a challenge no matter how hard we try. But it was a short Amtrak train, so it's already gone.

"Focus . . . It's mid-December, so there are little dead brown oak leaves all around me with bright-yellow leaves of a variety with which I'm not familiar gently sprinkled among them and still drifting down. The garden is mostly lush green with the exception of the bright-red footbridge spanning the neck of the pond that comes up under the porch where I am. The smell is musty and woodsy, and the sound of a water fountain in the middle of the pond permeates my senses and nearly drowns out the chatter of the birds and the chasing of squirrels. I can see the waterfall, though I can't hear it well. Little yellow leaves flutter and float all around there too. Soon I want to get up and walk the paths and hop across the stepping-stones in search of the multicolored koi that leisurely float or dart in the shallow leaf-covered water. I'm going to feel the thick moss at the water's edge that is saturated with the intensity of spring green even though it's winter—a reminder of new life to come. Then I plan to wind my way back to the camellia gardens in search of winter's first buds and blooms—the pinks and whites and reds. I'll be searching for peace and hope in the midst of it all. Maybe even a little joy and whichever other fruits of the Spirit that God sees fit to bestow upon me today, because spending time with Him isn't merely academic or life-enhancing. It's intended to be life-changing and rich, and it actually makes a difference in how you experience and feel about life and God and others. Devotional time is supposed to be practical.

"Being here in winter is different than summer, spring, or fall. Other times of year—especially in spring—you encounter children on field trips laughing and playing as their teachers lead them around the garden to show them God's handiwork. Even though that may not be the teacher's intentions, I still think God comes through to the children in some way. In the fall photographers often come here with high school seniors to take portraits to remember for a lifetime. And summer—well, everyone's here 'cause school is out. I used to be bothered when people interrupted my prayer time with their noises, but I eventually learned to look at the mommies with babbling babies in strollers and all the other passersby as wonderful examples of God's crowning act of creation and as illustrations of the wonder and complexity of being human.

"But today it's just me and nature and God. The groundskeepers aren't even here blowing and raking and telling jokes. So the setting is perfect and the timing is right. I'm going to close my computer and silence the phone and listen to the sounds and look at the sights and smell the scents that God has created just for me today. I'm going to walk with Him and talk with Him and I'm going to ask Him how His day is, and I'm sure He'll inquire about mine. As we spend some time in silence I'm sure my mind will be flooded with thoughts and ideas and little missions that He has for me, and perhaps I'll get some new ideas to write down here to share. I might even silently sing that old hymn "In the Garden" as I walk. That song is both classic and new. Classic because we've always sung it—and new because we've never done it. That's the weakness of the modern world—we have the knowledge but not the experience. I think one of the strengths of postmodernism is that it is more experiential in many ways.

"So my goal here this morning is to combine my relational understanding of God that I've found in Scripture with all the mulitsensory aspects of nature that He's surrounded us with, to help me enter into His very presence through the indwelling gift of the Holy Spirit. I'd like to suggest that you close your book as well and go find a quiet spot that's filled with sights and sounds and smells from God and talk to Him and ask Him to send the Holy Spirit to fill you and guide you too. He can handle talking to and filling us both at the same time. In fact, I think He likes it."

In the Garden

I come to the garden alone
While the dew is still on the roses
And the voice I hear falling on my ear
The Son of God discloses
And He walks with me, and He talks with me,
And He tells me I am His own;
And the joy we share as we tarry there,
None other has ever known.

He speaks, and the sound of His voice,
Is so sweet the birds hush their singing,
And the melody that He gave to me
Within my heart is ringing.
And He walks with me, and He talks with me,
And He tells me I am His own;
And the joy we share as we tarry there,
None other has ever known.

I'd stay in the garden with Him
Though the night around me be falling,
But He bids me go; through the voice of woe
His voice to me is calling.
And He walks with me, and He talks with me,
And He tells me I am His own;
And the joy we share as we tarry there,
None other has ever known.

—Charles Austin Miles (1912)

Wrapping Up the Gospel Commission According to John

Of the four gospel commissions, the one according to John is my favorite. Actually, everything according to John in the Bible is my favorite. I'm a sinner just like Peter, and I'm trying to figure out how to love Jesus better—just like Peter, too. I can't tell you where my devotional journey will end, because I hope it never does. I don't like doing the same old thing year after year. I enjoy new thoughts and feelings, and I want to grow. And

I don't have all the answers—in fact, I don't know that I have any. Instead, I have lots of questions. I can't wait to get to heaven for some solid answers and a great big, huge, giant bear hug from Jesus! I just want to disappear in His embrace and stay there forever . . . I think that's how David was feeling in Psalm 63 too. Perhaps then I will finally know the fullness of what love can be—right there in the arms of God. Care to join me?

Part II

Understanding Him Better

The Gospel Commission According to Luke: The Power of the Spirit

"It was . . . written that this message would be proclaimed in the authority of his name to all the nations, beginning in Jerusalem: 'There is forgiveness of sins for all who report.' You are witnesses of all these things. And now I will send the Holy Spirit, just as my Father promised. But stay here in the city until the Holy Spirit comes and fills you with power from heaven" (Luke 24:47-49).

In the gospel commission according to Luke the emphasis is to wait for the Holy Spirit to fill you before going into the world to witness. Who is the Holy Spirit? What does He do? How can we connect with Him and be filled by Him? In a world fascinated with the darker side of spiritual power, how can more people come to understand and be interested in the most elusive of the three Members of the Holy Trinity? Learning more about the Spirit can actually help you be more interested in knowing Jesus—the two are intimately intertwined and often inexplicably one.

Chapter 6

Of Ghosts and Spirits
and Otherworldly Beings

When I was a little kid, television had a cartoon program entitled *Casper the Friendly Ghost.* I just remember that he looked cuddly and cute and that the children in the cartoon liked him and thought he was their friend. People have been conditioned to be fascinated with ghosts and spirits and séances and Ouija boards and UFOs and all that otherworldly stuff since the beginning of time.

Seriously, think about what the media feeds us today, starting with the children's favorite—Disney. There is no longer any such thing as a Disney movie devoid of spirituality. Pocahontas consults with grandmother willow (a tree spirit). In *The Lion King* the son receives support and wisdom from his departed father. Just google "Disney" to find more. The *Harry Potter* series with its Hogwarts School of Witchcraft and Wizardry has taken the world by storm along with *Pirates of the Caribbean,* complete with skeletons marching across the bottom of the sea. Then there are the *Twilight* sagas, filled with good-looking, courteous, and of course very sexy vampires and werewolves. Why do they make Darth Vader and company so fascinatingly evil?

Such things are everywhere and so incredibly enticing and fascinating—who could resist?

The first supernatural appearance of an evil being on our planet was to Adam and Eve in the Garden of Eden when Lucifer himself morphed into the image of a beautiful serpent. He looked so sweet and lovely and spoke so nicely, offering eternal wisdom so convincingly, that he took down the entire human race in one fell swoop right there in front of the tree of the knowledge of good and evil—the very spot that Jesus had warned them to stay away from. At this point Adam and Eve were perfect and incredibly smart. How Satan pulled that trick off we'll never know this side of heaven, but it was definitely supernatural and sinister. Satan's had thousands of years to perfect his craft since that first seemingly innocent ethereal appearing. Watch out—he's very deceptive and sneaky, and Scripture says that he is still walking around like a roaring lion seeking those whom he can deceive and devour. Evil spirits are nothing to toy with!

Even King Saul, the first king of Israel, sought the spirit of the prophet Samuel through the witch of Endor despite the fact that God had specifically forbidden His people from consulting what He called "familiar spirits" (Lev. 19:31, NKJV). That was a huge mistake for Saul—he ended up talking to a demon and getting condemned by God instead of finding something cool, good, or fun. It wasn't a game!

Throughout the Gospels, Jesus constantly confronted demons and demon-possessed people. The demons harassed their hosts, even casting them into fire at times. Such entities were not nice or loving. They were terrifying. Family members would come to Jesus, begging for Him to free their loved ones from their power.

More recently shows such as *Crossing Over* claim to put people in contact with dead relatives right while you watch on TV. What could be nicer than talking to dear old grandma that you miss so much? Then, in the Wiccan movement, even witches are supposedly nice now rather than evil. Gone are the witches' brews for poisoning people, as well as evil spells. Wiccans just innocently worship mother earth now—whatever or whoever that is.

But if all the real miracle stories in the Bible of God's power are true—and I believe they are—why are people so fascinated with cheap and comparatively impotent fakes of the original Spirit of our holy God, known as the Holy Spirit or Holy Ghost? Why do we sell out so easily for phony imitations? Why are Christians today so out of touch with the true Spirit and power of God? Why can't we do something to help ourselves connect with the true Spirit of God rather than just take in whatever is offered to us spiritually?

I think a huge part of the problem is that Christianity has been around so long and has become so acceptable and watered down that people see it as a lifeless moral code that helps you to be a good person—end of story. The power is gone. Especially after the exposed deceptions of televangelists and fake faith healers working bogus miracles all in the name of the almighty dollar.

Let Me Tell You a Story—a Scary One

During one of my trips as a youth pastor, a number of young people showed up in my "chicken coop" on top of one of the houseboats we had rented on beautiful Lake Shasta. They had learned of some stories that I'd told the year before and now wanted them directly from me. But let me give you the background first.

The conversation they had heard about had started out with how the kids I was talking to claimed that they didn't believe in God and that there was no way to prove that He really existed. God just didn't seem to matter to them—they thought He was irrelevant. Keep in mind these were graduating seniors who came to church semiregularly and had attended Christian schools their whole lives—including daily Bible classes. So I went with the classic argument about origins—where did you come from if God didn't create you? It was a nice conversation, but it didn't matter to them where they came from or where they would go after they died. They were just concerned with the here and now and how to have fun. Now, let me say this—they were good respectful kids with honest questions. Neither argumentative nor rude, they were just thoroughly postmodern. After the typical approaches didn't work, somehow the Spirit led me to tell them scary stories. And the stories went like this . . .

Several years before, when I was a youth pastor in central California, one of the members of my young adult group became a student missionary at a Christian boarding academy on an Indian reservation in a nearby state. When he would come home on break, he would tell me amazing accounts of his experiences with the occult. Some of the non-Christian kids at the school would go home for weekend leaves and return possessed by demons—we're talking real-life no-joke demons! Their parents would take them to the medicine man or woman before sending them back to school. He said that he had personally walked into dorm rooms to find boys levitating right there before his eyes. At times when he was out late with the night watchman, they were chased around the gym by a glowing ball of light. They were being harassed by Satan's imps—for real! So one time when the young man was home visiting, he was so upset and scared that he asked me to have an anointing service for him. Gathering around him with a group of elders, we prayed for God's power to fill him and guide him and protect him, and then I anointed him with oil as instructed by the Bible. Later he said the demons never bothered him again after that. The Holy Spirit of the Christian God is the most powerful Spirit in the universe! Everyone else has to bow down and obey! That's my God!

I told the kids at Lake Shasta stories on the houseboat till 2:00 a.m.— every instance I knew of in which people had come to me because they were being harassed by demons and how the anointings stopped the harassment. One church member I was having Bible studies with described how in the middle of the night she would wake up terrified as she felt unseen hands pushing down on her chest so hard that she couldn't breathe. The hands would let up, then push—again and again. So we had another anointing service, and the supernatural being did not return.

A Native American girl I knew had a spirit that would visit her. She grew up raising her brothers and sisters on the reservation and had a lot of responsibility, because her parents were always gone. The being befriended her and made her feel good—for a while. Then it would start to harass her. We prayed for the demon to stay away and for Jesus to protect her, and I explained that no matter how lonely she might get, she mustn't talk to the spirit! When she ignored the spirit, it stayed away, but when she engaged it, it had control of her. Finally she learned to depend on Jesus, and she now lives a happy demon-free life!

Even though I hadn't seen the demonic activity myself, I was privileged to be a part of the heavenly activity on each person's behalf to drive out the evil spirits. Just listening to those true stories had been chilling for me when I first heard them, and then for the kids I told them to. Their eyes as wide as saucers, they exclaimed, "There really is something out there then!" It was incredible how evidence of evil spirits opened their hearts to the presence of the true Spirit of God, and they spread the word far and wide—so much so that kids were asking to hear the stories again the next year.

It's really sad when you realize that Christianity in America is so impotent that it lacks good miracle stories to help people believe in God. The accounts we've all heard from our grandparents and great-grandparents have worn off, because we haven't found our own miracle stories and experiences. Hand-me-down religion just doesn't work. Other people's stories can inspire us, but ultimately we have to find our own experience to make it real. If we have to resort to stories of the dark side to convince some people of God's power for now, so be it. I believe His power will be coming in force to America soon enough. Bible prophecy states that people will be healed and raised from the dead by God's power again before the end of time.

The final word is: Beware! Beware of what you familiarize yourself with. Do you want to be familiar with the spirits of the world and all its enticements, or would you rather become acquainted with the true God and His Spirit by engaging in a personal relationship with Jesus? We all must make choices. The decision is yours, and its results will be apparent before we know it and when we least expect it. At least that's what the Bible says.

Chapter 7

Who Is Your God?

Is your God—or the God you've been told about—always sweet and nice, or is He big and mean? Is your God watching you intently, just waiting for you to screw up so that He can pounce on you, or does He have a rubbery spine that stands for nothing and is so syrupy sweet that He lets you get away with anything? Is your God one inspired by popular culture, one inflicted on you as a child, or is He loving, kind, and desiring intimacy with you? Do you ever wonder if you know God as He really is or if you have a distorted view of Him?

The sad thing is that much of Christianity today believes in a weak God. Especially when we talk about the Holy Spirit, we usually refer to Him merely as the "Comforter." When I asked kids at one of my campus clubs this week what they thought about the Holy Spirit, they said that He is like your conscience, quietly whispering in your ear to do what is right. Well, those things are both true—but is that all He is? Jesus was kind and loving and helped lots of people and cried and hugged, but He also cut loose with some righteous indignation from time to time! For instance, when He cleared the Temple courtyard of dishonest money changers and merchants with a whip, He trashed their tables and threw stuff everywhere! He also got really upset at the Pharisees and Sadducees and called them names—hypocrites, liars, and thieves. Jesus always "says it like it is."

The Holy Spirit is sometimes hard to differentiate from Jesus and God—at least for me. But it seems as if They always work together in unison. When Jesus lived on earth, He was filled with the Holy Spirit, especially at His baptism. So the Holy Spirit was involved in all of Jesus' activities just as much as Christ Himself was. The Spirit must have participated in splitting the Red Sea and wiping out enemy armies when needed in the Old Testament, along with various other miracles in the Bible as well.

We must come to grips with the fact that the Bible tells us clearly that

God gave His followers superhuman strength and power to defeat their enemies. In those days people fought in brutal and bloody ways. It was either kill or be killed in those barbarous times. God did not allow David, the man after His own heart, to build a temple for Him, because he was an individual of blood and violence—through the power of the Holy Spirit. Not very comforting or warm and fuzzy, is it? But sometimes God needs to be strong to protect His children just as parents today would lay down their life if someone threatened their child.

Deuteronomy 18:9-14 reveals the fact that God ordered the Israelites to wipe out whole cities and peoples when they went in to take over the Promised Land, because the people already inhabiting the land had completely given themselves over to evil. So we can assume that in abandoning themselves to such horrible satanic activities that they had effectively committed the unpardonable sin and sealed their own fate—that there was no hope for them. If God had allowed them to live, they would have lured His children into the same sins. So God destroyed these followers of the devil in order to protect His own. They had made their choice and suffered its consequences. Satan is the father of all evil people, and thankfully God will deal with the devil one day—He and His Spirit.

David creates an amazingly powerful picture of God in Psalm 18. If we ever want to get out of lukewarm Christianity, we need to embrace the powerful side of our God as well as the comforting side. David wrote the psalm after the Lord gave him victory over Saul and all his enemies. Check it out:

> "The ropes of death entangled me;
>   floods of destruction swept over me.
> The grave wrapped its ropes around me;
>   death laid a trap in my path.
> But in my distress I cried out to the Lord;
>   yes, I prayed to my God for help.
> He heard me from his sanctuary;
>   my cry to him reached his ears.
> Then the earth quaked and trembled.
> The foundations of the mountains shook;
>   they quaked because of his anger.
> Smoke poured from his nostrils;
>   fierce flames leaped from his mouth.

Glowing coals blazed forth from him.
He opened the heavens and came down;
dark storm clouds were beneath his feet.
Mounted on a mighty angelic being, he flew,
soaring on the wings of the wind.
He shrouded himself in darkness,
veiling his approach with dark rain clouds.
Thick clouds shielded the brightness around him
And rained down hail and burning coals.
The Lord thundered from heaven;
the voice of the Most High resounded
amid the hail and burning coals.
He shot his arrows and scattered his enemies;
his lightning flashed, and they were greatly confused.
Then at your command, O Lord,
at the blast of your breath,
the bottom of the sea could be seen,
and the foundations of the earth were laid bare.
He reached down from heaven and rescued me;
he drew me out of deep waters.
He rescued me from my powerful enemies,
from those who hated me and were too strong for me."
—Ps. 18:4-17

I read that to my campus clubs this week, and the students' eyes grew wide! They'd never heard of that kind of God. They only knew about the boring God that's never captured their imagination.

What about you? Have you ever pictured God with smoke pouring out of his nostrils or flames coming out of His mouth as He rides an angel while shooting arrows and raining down fiery hail? This is not the still small voice we seek in the quiet, is it? I wonder how David experienced God. How much time did he spend with Him in the quiet and how much on the battlefield? David wrote beautifully intimate psalms to his God and would lie awake at night dreaming about Him, and then went out to slaughter his thousands and ten thousands as the maidens sang when he returned home victorious.

Maybe the psalm is metaphor. Or maybe it isn't. Somewhere back in the 1990s I remember reading one of the first Christian novels to hit the bookstores. Called *This Present Darkness,* its theme was spiritual warfare. The captivating thing was that the author, Frank Peretti, attempted to pull back the curtain to let us see behind the scenes of the struggle between good and evil. In doing so, Peretti described in detail the good and bad angels fighting over people in the midst of decision-making moments. He attempted to portray in new ways the old image of the good angel sitting on one shoulder of a conflicted individual and the evil one on the other. Peretti gave the angels voices and appearances and had them chasing each other and celebrating their victories.

Now, we all believe in guardian angels, don't we? Have you ever tried to picture them? We believe in demons, too. The Bible is quite specific about their existence, and Jesus cast many out during His earthly ministry. Scripture even describes the contortions on the faces of those possessed by such beings. War broke out in heaven, and good angels fought against evil ones. What do you think such conflict looked like? Even Ellen White claimed that it was terribly difficult to describe heavenly scenes with human words. Maybe Psalm 18 is actually David's best attempt at describing what he literally saw God doing while helping him win one of his battles. Think about it—what does it look like when the battle is won by the Lord? Remember when God opened the eyes of Elijah's servant and allowed him to see the fiery chariots of the Lord that would conquer the enemy? It left him completely shocked and in awe!

When we visualize angels, most people typically think of the idyllic paintings of blond-haired men in white robes with birds' wings mounted on their backs—not exactly armed for battle, are they? And in the Bible it's true that many times angels take on human form for their visits so that they don't scare us to death. Well, I'm not trying to destroy or alter that image for you, but check out Ezekiel's portrayal of what the angels he saw looked like:

"From the center of the cloud came four living beings that looked human, except that each had four faces and four wings. Their legs were straight, and their feet had hooves like those of a calf and shone like burnished bronze. Under each of their four wings I could see human hands.... The wings of each living being touched the wings of the beings beside it. Each one moved straight forward in any direction without turning around. Each had a human face in the front, the face of a lion on the right side, the face of an ox on the left side, and the face of an eagle at the back.... The living beings looked like bright coals of fire or brilliant torches, and lightning seemed to flash back and forth among them. And the living beings darted to and fro like flashes of lightning.

"As I looked at these beings, I saw four wheels on the ground beside them, one wheel belonging to each. The wheels sparkled as if made of beryl. All four wheels looked alike and were made the same; each wheel had a second wheel turning crosswise within it. The beings could move in any of the four directions they faced, without turning as they moved. The rims of the four wheels were tall and frightening, and they were covered with eyes all around. . . . As they flew, their wings sounded to me like waves crashing against the shore, or like the voice of the Almighty or like the shouting of a mighty army" (Eze. 1:5-24).

I've quoted only part of the passage here. Why not open your Bible right now and check out the rest? The prophet sees the angels as stationed below the very throne of God Himself.

Many places in the Bible describe God as mighty and powerful. Another great and awesome picture of God appears in Exodus when He spoke the Ten Commandments to the children of Israel. Look at the context of the commandments in Exodus 20. That means examine the verses both before and after them. The end of Exodus 19 says that God descended on the mountain in the form of fire (verse 18), and because of the fire, smoke billowed everywhere. A huge earthquake accompanied the fire and smoke, and horns blasted loudly. The Lord told Moses to keep the children of Israel off the mountain or they would die! But what is especially interesting is what happened after God spoke the Ten Commandments.

The Bible says that the people begged Moses never to let God speak to them again, because they were so afraid. Then at that same moment Moses very peacefully and calmly explained that God wasn't going to destroy them—He was just showing them His power. He told them not to be afraid and to let their newfound respect for God remind them to keep from sinning. I'm sure that scene was so emblazoned in their minds that they were on their best behavior for at least a couple of days! But the really awesome part is that then, "as the people stood in the distance, Moses approached the dark cloud where God was" (Ex. 20:21).

The former slaves, fresh from captivity, had completely forgotten about God and didn't know Him. They were afraid, but Moses, who knew Him as his best friend and confidant, joyfully walked into the presence of His God to spend time with Him. That's what John is talking about when he states that "such love has no fear, because perfect love expels all fear. If we are afraid, it is for fear of punishment, and this shows that we have not experienced his perfect love. We love each other, because he loved us first" (1 John 4:18, 19).

What that means is that fear is only for people who either hate God or have refused to get to know Him. But people who love God and have a relationship with Him won't be afraid. They will be in awe of Him and filled with His power in amazing ways as happened to the disciples when they went out to preach and heal in Jesus' name after receiving the Holy Spirit at Pentecost.

Even though God is powerful, that doesn't make Him mean. Some people portray Him as a harsh taskmaster over His own people. But we are not saved or lost by what we do. Rather, we are saved or lost by whom we choose to know and follow. God is not out to punish everyone on the planet —only those who choose to persistently stand against Him—and then it's as a disciplinary measure in hopes of correcting them and convincing them to choose Him instead.

God's power is mighty and awesome, and when you sense the Holy Spirit filling you and His strength surging through you, it's the most amazing feeling in the world. I know because I've felt it myself, and so have countless other people throughout earth's history. Worship Him who sustains the universe "by the mighty power of his command" (Heb. 1:3). God is not only love but power, too, and He wants to live in you and work through you via the indwelling presence of the Holy Spirit.

Chapter 8

Cats in the Sheep Pen

It's only by the grace of God that I did not die from breaking my neck as I dove headfirst into the shallow end of a pool—drunk and naked in the wee hours of the morning after a health club Christmas party at the age of 24. It was a miracle that my neck merely jammed instead of snapping under the weight of my 215 pounds. The resultant headache was incredible. And it's another miracle that I went on to drive home safely that night without killing anyone with my car or getting killed in an accident myself. When I woke up in the morning I had no recollection of returning home, and when I looked out the window I found my car parked half up on the curb and almost into a tree. It wasn't the first time that I couldn't remember driving home, and, unfortunately, it wouldn't be the last. And it's a miracle that during that phase of my young adulthood, as I was searching for meaning in life, one night God gave me a dream that I wouldn't always be a drunken fool but would instead be a preacher or evangelist proclaiming His love to the world. What a God of grace, vision, and destiny. Thank You, Jesus!

I believe it was the Holy Spirit of God along with my guardian angel that watched over me and performed miracles on my behalf to save my life countless times from my reckless lifestyle. I don't know how they coordinated it all, but it is only by the power of the Spirit working in my life that I'm here today. I don't know why the Spirit chose to protect me and call me to His work, but I do know that my grandmother prayed for me every day until she died. Thank You, Jesus, for a godly, Spirit-filled grandmother!

So you see that I've been on both sides of the spirit world. For many years now I've lived wholeheartedly for Jesus by the power of His indwelling Spirit—but before He called me out of the world I lived for myself and my desires and was speeding down the path to the dark side even though I hadn't intentionally chosen it. Since Adam and Eve sinned, we are all born into sin. Unless we willfully choose to leave it, we are stuck there, a slave to its powers.

A dysfunctional religion that emphasized regulations and behavior rather than a personal relationship with Jesus Himself had nurtured my path to near destruction. Rules devoid of relationship are a recipe for sure disaster in one ditch or the other—angry legalistic conformity or a discounting and distancing from anything that smacks of religion. I'm close to people who've split in both directions, and know of only a few who are still in the middle—most are still searching even if they're still in the relative safety of the church.

I don't blame a bit of this on my parents. Good, kind, and well-meaning, they merely followed the prescribed method of spirituality of the day. When my wife and I attend her academy reunions, we find that only a very small minority of her classmates still have any regular contact with church. In my own Facebook academy reunions it appears that most of my class has moved on as well. It's a miracle that we have any church left at all. Stories similar to mine abound from coast to coast. It seems that for generations our churches have had the form of godliness but have lacked the power to truly change lives. The church remains only because of the grace of God, who still cherishes it as the apple of His eye and as His chosen institution for reaching the world. But even though it exists, the church is struggling to relate to the people of the twenty-first century as revealed by the analogy of the cats in the sheep pen. And it goes like this . . .

The Analogy of the Cats in the Sheep Pen

Once upon a time there was a cat in a sheep pen. Now, it used to be that back in Jesus' day and even up until the first part of the twentieth century people primarily used sheep pens for keeping sheep. But today more and more frequently churches are trying to use sheep pens to keep cats in, and it's really not working out very well. The cats just jump out and run away! And some of them even dare to sit on a sheep and take a nap before they take off (and I actually have a picture of this to prove it!). And even though the cats typically look young, sweet, and innocent, and the sheep usually appear old and grumpy, that's not necessarily the case.

The Bible has lots of stories that refer to the Israelites as a flock of sheep—such as when God brought them out of slavery in Egypt. The Bible says in Psalm 78:52: "But he led his own people like a flock of sheep, guiding them safely through the wilderness." Jews were very corporate—they had a flock/herd mentality—and the entire population wandered in the wilderness together. When Jesus walked the earth huge crowds followed Him, listening to His teachings and watching for miracles. And then we see the fickleness of the crowds and the herd mentality as those same people who had apparently loved Jesus quickly turned on Him and joined the Pharisees' crowd in chanting "crucify Him."

And that's how it used to be up until a few years ago in the Christian church—it was "all for one and one for all." I remember about 12 years ago when we had a work bee at my church to remove all the pews so that we could put in new carpet, and the only people that showed up to help were those from the World War II generation. They had a great team spirit, and not one from that generation still able to work was missing. Several times they asked me why they were the only ones there.

My wife loves to tell stories from when she was a girl (not that many years ago) about the church socials she used to attend. She said that everyone would show up and bring 15 to 20 flavors of homemade ice cream. Everyone would play softball and have a good time. And that's how church socials and potlucks were when I was a kid too. At our church potlucks the dessert table was bigger than the entrée table—it was the greatest thing a kid could hope for. Whenever the flock was called together, it seemed that all the sheep were present, and they all brought the best they had to share.

But today it appears that there aren't many sheep left in the world, and the ones that are here are growing older. And at the same time the cat population seems to be getting out of control! Cats are independent, giving attention and affection on their terms and in their way, regardless of what you may want from them. They don't do anything simply because everyone else is doing it or because someone expects them to. Instead of traveling in large herds, they go about in small packs called prides if you are a lion, colonies if you're of the feral cat persuasion, or in twos, threes, and fours if you're the housecat type. That's why young "cats" don't come to church work bees, socials, or potlucks either. Their generation is decidedly missing because they're off doing whatever seems important to them as individuals or in smaller groups. Coming and going as they please, they observe the rules they like and ignore the ones they don't. Do you know any "cat people"? Are you one?

The problem is that we, as church people, are trying to keep cats in pens designed to house sheep, and that's difficult to do because cats prefer to be free and independent, making their own choices and leading their own lives regardless of what the rest of the flock may be doing. The Bible has no parables of the lost cat, because cats are never lost! In the movies they can make amazing odysseys across the country to get home. Ferals are never lost either—they just live wherever they are. And if a cat really was lost, it would never admit it. They live to be free!

The postmodern dilemma is how do we keep cats in the sheepfold? How does a farm built for sheep transition to raising cats? How does a church structure intended for people with a group mentality relate to people from an increasingly individualistic society?

I grew up in a church with lots of sheep-oriented rules and regulations, and that seems to have worked for the older people but not for me. My generation called all the rules the "do's and don'ts," and I've heard stories from people across the country lamenting the "legalism" that they had to endure as kids. The structure that used to keep people in the church and to give them a feeling of belonging and a sense of right and wrong started driving people out of the church in my day, because people and the society we live in have changed, as well as how we think and act. And so the church we all know and love needs to find ways to become meaningful for people once again.

As we discussed at the beginning of this section, I believe that Christianity today seems irrelevant to many people because we have forgotten how powerful God really is, and because we have come to rely on a "system" of spirituality to save us rather than a personal relationship with the Creator of the universe. I just love reading Psalm 104, which talks about God's creative power and how He scooped out the valleys with His hands and piled up the mountains with the might of His power. It speaks about how He feeds all animals and watches over His entire creation. Although mighty and powerful, He wants to have a personal relationship with every creature He has made—including you and me! It thrills me to know that I'm not merely a number in a system—but a precious child of the King of the universe! This concept alone has transformed my personal spirituality and brought healing, hope, and love into my life. And it has given me a mission as well—one founded in the great gospel commission.

Matthew 10:16 says: "Look, I am sending you out as sheep among wolves. So be as shrewd as snakes and harmless as doves." God has in fact sent us out on a mission to reach the world with His gospel, and He has the power to perform miracles through us, just as He did through the disciples when He commissioned them long ago. While we go out as individuals and in small groups to work for Him and be used by Him, we find safety and encouragement in the flock. We need each other's strengths to help over-come our own individual weaknesses. But most of all we require a Savior to lead us as the good shepherd that He is. Furthermore, He empowers us with His strength through the Spirit that surges through us and into the world around us just as He has done through all of His disciples since the beginning of time.

God has commanded all people of all generations to fulfill the gospel commission. But our world is no longer the same one it was 100 years ago, because the people in it have undergone great cultural shifts, and we ourselves may respond to the gospel differently than those before us did. As a result, we may need to mix up our devotional lives a bit in order to understand the ways that God wants to communicate with us today. But no matter how we connect with other people, we can do it powerfully only through the strength of the Holy Spirit.

Everyone from every era needs to engage Scripture as part of their devotional times. But maybe you'll want to add some multisen-sory aspects for a fuller experience—such as the tastes and smells from the sanctuary that we mentioned in a previous chapter. Remember the quote from Ellen White that said to spend an hour a day imag-ining the scenes of Jesus' life? I think we still need to do that to-day, and also to find new ways to engage all of Scripture as well. Such multimedia devotions as watching praise and worship songs on YouTube can be good from time to time as well.

The goal of this book is to help you to try lots of devotional options in order to find your way closer to the One who is the powerful lover of your soul.

Chapter 9

The Spirit of Power and Love

We encounter God's power through His love. In Psalm 18 we saw that David experienced the Lord's amazing power in response to his desperate cry to the Deity whom he knew and loved. And even though in this section we are specifically looking at the power of the Holy Spirit promised in the gospel commission according to Luke, keep in mind that the Father, Son, and Holy Spirit are one. Any evidence of love and power that we see in one member of the Trinity we will find in all of Them. With that in mind, let's take a look at how God sends His power into our lives through His love as seen in Ephesians 3:14-19. The heading in my Bible for this section of Scripture is "Paul's Prayer for Spiritual Growth."

"When I think of all this, I fall to my knees and pray to the Father, the Creator of everything in heaven and on earth. I pray that from his glorious, unlimited resources he will empower you with inner strength through his Spirit. Then Christ will make his home in your hearts as you trust in him. Your roots will grow down into God's love and keep you strong. And may you have the power to understand, as all God's people should, how wide, how long, how high, and how deep his love is. May you experience the love of Christ, though it is too great to understand fully. Then you will be made complete with all the fullness of life and power that comes from God."

Now, let's go through this passage one verse at a time so that we can understand more about how God works to use His power and love in our lives to draw us close to Him, protect and nurture us, and give us the great lives that He wants all of us to have. This is far deeper than any "system" of religion.

"When I think of all this, I fall to my knees and pray to the Father, the Creator of everything in heaven and on earth" (verses 14, 15). Here we need to determine the context of the passage. It is always important

54

to look over the verses around a particular verse of Scripture so that you understand why the biblical author says what he does. The context of this passage appears in verses 1-14. In it Paul speaks about God's "mysterious plan" being revealed (verse 3). It is that all of God's people—not just the Jews—can all share equally in the riches that God offers when one accepts the gospel (verse 6). Before this time the Jews thought they were the only ones who could go to heaven. But after Jesus' crucifixion He directed His followers to take the gospel to the entire world so that anyone who would believe in God could be saved. That's great news for people like me who aren't Jewish. I'm a Gentile, and I'm so thankful that the gospel is for me, too! Then Paul mentions the privilege he has because God has chosen him to present this good news to the entire world and that the "church," composed of all God's people, is the organization to work through in doing so (verse 10).

This is what Paul has in mind when he says that he falls to his knees and prays to the Creator every time he thinks of his amazing opportunity to share such a wonderful gift with the world.

"I pray that from his glorious, unlimited resources he will empower you with inner strength through his Spirit" (verse 16). What could God's glorious unlimited resources be that help us to grow in strength? Should we get a good deal on a house or a car, we tend to call it a blessing from God or say that we were blessed. But what about the seemingly good people who didn't receive such things? Did God curse them for some reason? The psalmist and countless people since his time have wondered why God would apparently curse good people and bless the wicked.

What can God's unlimited resources be that give us mighty inner strength through His Spirit? Good things don't bring strength—they are more capable of giving joy. However, the book of James tells us that God allows trials and temptations to enter our lives to help us grow in strength. But how can we consider trials and temptations glorious, unlimited resources when they are not?

Can it be that God Himself is the glorious unlimited resource? It is only His love received and experienced through intimate communion with Him that can sustain us through the trials of life. And it is true that His love knows no limits. Trials are never glorious—only Jesus Christ is, and through the mighty power of His Spirit anything He touches can become glorious as well. We should not exalt in trials—only in Jesus. Then—and only then—the trials become useful for helping us grow.

The context of this verse clearly tells us that we survive the trials of this world by putting sturdy roots down into the soil of God's love that is so wide and long and deep that it can encapsulate and consume any trouble the devil might throw our way. And it is especially in the times of trouble that we can fully experience and understand the love that Jesus so freely offers us. Notice that it is specifically the Spirit that delivers this strength in cooperation with Jesus and the Father.

"Then Christ will make his home in your hearts as you trust in him" (verse 17). What comes to mind when you hear the word "home"? I think of acceptance, warmth, love, joy, and hugs. That's not to say those are the things I experience every time I go home—no one does—but those are the good parts. Those are the things I want home to be. No matter who you are or how good or bad your life may be, we all have an ideal home that we long for. Jesus wants to make that home in your heart. As God Himself— the most glorious, unlimited resource in the universe—comes into your heart, He brings with Him all the love that makes Him who He is.

All of us have been hurt at some time in our lives—sometimes by the people we love most. We all need something outside of ourselves to cling to that can give us hope to live and carry on. Well, God wants to bring His love that is outside of ourselves into each of us to dwell there and give us the peace and hope and strength we need. The power of the God of the universe can dwell in your heart if only you will allow Him in. It is as we learn to trust Him and invite Him in that we begin to experience it for ourselves.

"Your roots will grow down into God's love and keep you strong" (verse 17). Roots hold plants in place and are the system they use for gathering water and nutrients to remain healthy and even flourish. It is how we cling to the rock of our salvation and how we grow strong in our faith. There is no better way to be nurtured and to flourish than to feed on God's love. But we need to grasp how huge God's love is when we begin to sink our roots down into it. The next verse explains this in an incredible way.

"And may you have the power to understand, as all God's people should, how wide, how long, how high, and how deep his love is" (verse 18). Why does it take "power"? Does it mean that we can't understand God before we give ourselves to Him? Scripture says that Jesus died to save us even while we were yet sinners—before we could even turn our own lives around. As I shared earlier, it was while I was still a drunken fool that God gave me a vision of His love for me and showed me the plan He had for my life. I didn't come to him—He came to me first, as He does for us all. Just as

Jesus appeared to Saul on the road to Damascus He seeks out every one of us to call us to be His own.

Now, here is the incredible part. God's love is wide and long and high and deep! It is huge! In fact, it encapsulates the universe. There is nowhere you can run to get away from divine love. You can escape from it only by persistent denial and deliberate attempts to be rid of it. While that is difficult, sadly it is possible. We call it the unpardonable sin, as we mentioned earlier. People who have committed the unpardonable sin are typically downright evil, because they have given themselves over to the devil himself. The unpardonable sin is irreversible, but it is hard to commit. Yet once a person does arrive at that point, they have absolutely no desire to reverse it. So don't worry: if you've gotten this far into this book, you have definitely not committed that sin. God's love is still here surrounding you, encapsulating you, protecting you, and wanting to permeate you to the very core of your being.

"May you experience the love of Christ, though it is too great to understand fully. Then you will be made complete with all the fullness of life and power that comes from God" (verse 19). Here is the part that was missing from my life as a kid. I never "experienced" Christ's love. While I heard about behaviors and beliefs, I had never been led into a relationship with Jesus. Well, I suppose I had some experiences such as my baptism, in which at 11 years of age I felt God's presence so fully that as I came up out of the water I just wanted to go and be with Jesus in heaven right then. I can remember a few isolated experiences like that, but overall I grew up with religious doctrines, not spiritual experiences. It's sad that things had to be that way. Apparently no one had ever read this text that is so clear. The verse says that we can never fully understand it no matter how much we study it or slice and dice various passages of Scripture to try to explain it. God's love defies explanation—it must be experienced to be grasped!

Now, that doesn't mean we don't try to understand Scripture—we are obviously doing a lot of that in this book. But Paul clearly explains here that it is only when we actually encounter God's love that we will be made complete and be able to enjoy all the fullness of life that He has in store for us. Only then will we receive the power that God wants to bring to our lives. Are you ready to give it a try? Do you want your life to be complete? Do you want to open your heart up to Jesus and the indwelling of His Spirit on a daily basis and become a new creature full of His strength, power, and love? Jesus offers you this gift—it is waiting for you now.

Chapter 10

Being Reborn of the Spirit

For God loved the world so much that he gave his one and only Son, so that everyone who believes in him will not perish but have eternal life."

John 3:16 is arguably the most famous passage in the Bible. We see it everywhere from bumper stickers to billboards to banners at football games. Most people can recite it—and yet they don't really know it very well. Do you know who spoke the words of John 3:16 or whom they were addressed to? Did you know that the verses right before it talk about a snake? This world-famous verse has become a cliché with very little meaning for most people. So let's take a little time right now to try to dig a little deeper into this iconic verse and see the treasures that it holds.

Jesus spoke the words of John 3:16 about Himself in the middle of a discussion He was having with Nicodemus about the Holy Spirit and how the Spirit gives birth to spiritual life (why we are discussing the verse here). Now, I'm sure most of you know the story of Jesus' conversation late at night with this well-known and wealthy leader in Israel. Even though the rest of the leaders of Israel later had to hire Judas to betray to them Jesus' whereabouts at night, somehow Nicodemus was able to find Him all by himself so that no one would know he had sought Him out. Nicodemus came to Jesus confessing that he believed Him to be a teacher sent from God.

The religious leader was barely two lines into his greeting when Jesus cut him off and said: "I tell you the truth, unless you are born again, you cannot see the Kingdom of God" (verse 3). They are serious words that we should not take lightly. Speaking to a good man caught up in the height of religious legalism, Jesus explains to him that unless a person is reborn of water and the Spirit he cannot understand spiritual things or be saved. When Jesus taught His disciples to pray, He said: "May your Kingdom come soon. May your will be done on earth, as it is in heaven" (Matt.

6:10), indicating that part of Jesus' mission was to bring the kingdom of God close enough to earth for people to see it and desire to be a part of it.

Jesus' presence on earth was what attracted people to God's kingdom and gave them a desire for more. So what Jesus was saying to Nicodemus in John 3:3 was that the religious leader would neither be able to notice the kingdom of God being established on earth nor recognize the will of God for his life unless he was first born of the Spirit. And the same is true for us today. Unless we are born of the Holy Spirit we won't be able to distinguish true spirituality from false spirituality or legalistic religion from a heartfelt relationship with Jesus. The Spirit is the one who convicts us and draws us, and unless we respond to that influence, we cannot know God. But the Spirit is as elusive as the wind and can be difficult to grasp. Because of that, the Father sent Jesus into the world to work together with the Holy Spirit by being the visible manifestation of the Trinity. Spirituality is a mystery indeed, because it has no human origin—it is a true manifestation of the unsearchable God of the universe who spoke our world into existence and holds all power in heaven and on earth in His hands. It is something that we will be trying to understand for the rest of our lives and then through-out the ceaseless ages of eternity.

God sent Jesus to put a face on divinity. Christ came to reveal the Spirit to us, tell us about the Father, and demonstrate in person His love for us. He showed that love by teaching us how to live and then by dying in our place—the place that we deserve because of our sins—so that we can share a place with Him in heaven. Finally, just before Jesus left earth to return to His Father in heaven, He told the disciples that He would pour the Spirit out on them to make it possible for them to carry the gospel to the ends of the earth. Without the Spirit they would be powerless, and without the Spirit we are powerless as well. And now it is the Spirit who teaches us through Scripture that the Father loved us so much that He sent His only Son so that whoever chooses to believe in Him doesn't have to die. It is through the power of the Spirit that we can have eternal life!

Spirit's role

Now, just in case this seems a bit confusing, we are going to try to simplify it just a little bit. The apostle John, who recorded John 3:16 and the story around it, also wrote the epistles of John, and in his first epistle he comments and elaborates on John 3:16. Here is what he says:

"God showed how much he loved us by sending his one and only Son into the world so that we might have eternal life through him. This is real love—not that we loved God, but that he loved us and sent his Son as a sacrifice to take away our sins. Dear friends, since God loved us that much, we surely ought to love each other. No one has ever seen God. But if we love each other, God lives in us, and his love is brought to full expression in us. And God has given us his Spirit as proof that we live in him and he in us" (1 John 4:9-13).

Jesus Christ, the greatest gift our world has ever received, went back to heaven knowing that He would continue to dwell in us and work through us till the end of time by means of the Spirit. Did you notice the last phrase in the passage? It states that the presence of the Spirit is proof that God is living in us. Jesus and the Spirit are one, and They are also one with the Father. They all love us and all want to live with us for eternity so that They are all three involved in reaching down from heaven to save us. Now let's go ahead and try to wrap up this somewhat difficult concept.

Wrapping Up the Gospel Commission According to Luke

If God was easy to understand, He would be little more than the invention of human minds just as the ancient Greek or other gods. But the fact that He is complex and difficult to grasp is proof that He is otherworldly and real! The Lord is mighty and awesome in His power and in His love, and He somehow blends both the power and the love together perfectly. He can hold you gently in one hand while protecting you from a nuclear blast with the other. And God is one even though He comes in three parts. The Trinity—the three in one—is one of the most helpful concepts for trying to understand the Holy Spirit and His role in our lives.

The Father, Son, and Spirit are one in thought and purpose. The Father is the one to whom we often address our prayers, the one who sent Jesus to earth, and the one who sends the Spirit to help us as well. It can be confusing to separate the Three. Therefore, when we discuss one of Them, we actually talk about Them all. That is why we spoke of the Father, Son, and Spirit nearly equally in this section on the Holy Spirit. Because they cannot function separately, They are one. This is good news for us—it's the best three for one deal in the universe!

So keep in mind that as we pursue our relationship with our powerful and loving Creator, Sustainer, and Redeemer we sometimes talk to Him as Jesus and sometimes as God the Father, because they are both God and are both involved in our lives, but it is the Spirit that delivers the power of God to us to live in us. That is why Jesus told His disciples to wait for the Spirit before going "into all the world" (Mark 16:15).

Yes, it is a difficult concept, but in the end just remember that what is important is that we recognize that we are completely submersed in and surrounded by the love of the Father, Son, and Spirit both together and separately. To God be the glory and honor for ever and ever. Amen!

Part III

Receiving His Word

The Gospel Commission According to Matthew: Teaching and Discipling

"Jesus came and told His disciples, 'I have been given all authority in heaven and on earth. Therefore, go and make disciples of all the nations, baptizing them in the name of the Father and the Son and the Holy Spirit. Teach these new disciples to obey all the commands I have given you. And be sure of this: I am with you always, even to the end of the age'" (Matt. 28:18-20).

After drawing you to Christ's love, the Spirit begins to help you to understand Scripture as you never have before. Then, as you learn more, the Spirit fills you and compels you to share the love and peace that you've found in a better understanding of Jesus. At this point the Spirit not only draws but also fills you and sends you forth with power to make disciples. You cannot teach people about Jesus effectively if you do not understand Him yourself. Teaching and discipling are as intimately intertwined as Jesus and the Spirit, and as Jesus and you by the power of the Spirit. Effective teaching can never stand alone. It comes in the context of discipling relationships—Jesus discipling you and you discipling someone else—all through the power of the Spirit. In this section we will look at examples of how to understand Scripture devotionally and apply it to our personal relationships with Jesus.

Chapter 11

Why Do We Have Bibles, and What Should We Do With Them?

David didn't have a Bible. Most people he knew didn't either. And David never sat on the hillside reading his handy-dandy devotional book from XYZ publisher for 10 minutes every morning before he went out to watch his sheep, thinking that was all he needed to do to connect with God. In fact, David might not have even been able to read. Scrolls were few and far between. Bibles weren't available to the average person until the time of the Protestant Reformation in the 1500s! Have you ever wondered how people had devotions before there were Bibles?

When David composed his psalms they were just poetry and songs coming from his heart. He gave them as a gift to his Lord as he lay there thinking about Him—such as Psalm 63. He may even be surprised when he gets to heaven to find out that his psalms became many people's favorite part of Scripture. David's psalms were merely the by-product of his relationship with Jesus. But I'm glad they were written down to share with us and show us how to connect with God ourselves.

I'm sure David must have heard the books of Moses being read at the sanctuary—or at least the oral traditions being recited. Back in David's day people got their copy of Scripture by putting it into their minds, where no one could take it away. It couldn't be lost unless they stopped reciting it and it faded from their memory. So when we pray through scriptures that we've memorized, we may be having our devotions a lot like David did. He probably had the scribes write his psalms down as he recited them once he became king years later. That's one conversation I want to have with him when we get to heaven—I want to know how he did it and what it felt like.

The point I'm making here is that most people in David's day and the common people in Jesus' time couldn't sit down and pull out their scrolls to read their devotions or get into proof-texting arguments over what the details of each passage meant. They focused more on the story line rather than the detailed meaning of each word. And as we read Scripture we find that the most profound thing about Jesus' life on earth was not His teachings themselves—it was the way He lived them out in His life. Teachings must be put into practice if they are to be effective. Jesus was Immanuel, "God is with us"—loving us, holding us, healing us. And it is our lives that should be speaking to the world—witnessing far more powerfully than our words.

Even Paul just wrote his letters in the New Testament to people—individuals and groups with all sorts of issues that he was trying to help them with. Someone would stand up and read the letter while everyone else listened. It wasn't until later, as some of the Church Fathers decided to become elite intellectuals and to try to compete with Greek philosophy, that modern theology developed. Sometimes I wish we didn't have theology, because it's so divisive—but we do need it, and I'm glad we have theologians who actually know what they are doing, because a lot of common people who try to get into it just really mess it up and get distracted from what they really need. What we must have from the Bible first and foremost is for it to help us in our devotional lives by nurturing our personal relationships with Jesus. Without that in place our theology will always be a mess!

So the focus of this section is not on theology at all—it's on reading the Bible devotionally. And that's what I'd like to talk about here, because a devotional approach to Scripture will win a lot more souls to Jesus than theology will. Winning souls is what the gospel commission is all about in Matthew—teachings that make people want to be disciples of Jesus. And we all know Jesus Himself won people with love and tenderness—not with theological treatises and arguments. His teachings were never complicated. Even children could understand them. Theology and the prophecies of Daniel and Revelation have been effective in evangelism when they were being presented to people who were already Christians. Theology is good at clarifying your relationship with Jesus, but if you don't have Him first, it can just be confusing.

Because of an overwhelming focus on theology in the past we in many ways have forgotten how to present the basic gospel of Jesus. That's why so many kids are being lost from the church today. Theology alone doesn't make faithful disciples. Our goal should be not to master the Bible, but to use it to master a relationship with Jesus. Let's take a look at what discovering Him did for one of the most legalistic Bible scholars of all time—Saul of Tarsus.

When he referred back to his old life in Philippians 3:5, 6, Paul (his new name) said: "I am . . . a real Hebrew if ever there was one! I was a member of the Pharisees, who demand the strictest obedience to the Jewish law. I was so zealous that I harshly persecuted the church. And as for righteousness, I obeyed the law without fault."

Paul knew the law if anyone ever did—at least he knew the words of the law. But he didn't know the One who had inspired it. As a result he persecuted the very ones who were truly following God. It wasn't until Paul encountered Jesus on the road to Damascus that his viewpoint changed. Once he met Jesus personally, it took only a short time for him to think back through the scriptures that he already knew and reinterpret them properly and become a passionate follower of Jesus! Knowing Him makes all the difference when it comes to understanding Scripture.

So let's look at some passages that you probably already know and try to interpret them devotionally—in light of a relationship with Jesus. You may be surprised at what we find. Let's start out with the very law itself—the Ten Commandments as found in Exodus 20.

Using the Ten Commandments to Nurture Your Relationship With Jesus

Back in chapter 7 we talked about how God appeared at Mount Sinai to tell His children about the Ten Commandments. We noted that He and His awesome display of power in the form of fire, smoke, and earthquake had frightened the people. Terrified, they don't want God to speak to them personally anymore. But Moses eagerly walked into the darkness to be with his Lord. In Psalm 19 we see that David had developed a relationship with God like Moses had. David loved God and His law. He said:

> "The instructions of the Lord are perfect,
>   reviving the soul.
> The decrees of the Lord are trustworthy,
>   making wise the simple.
> The commandments of the Lord are right,
>   bringing joy to the heart.
> The commands of the Lord are clear,
>   giving insight for living.
> Reverence for the Lord is pure,
>   lasting forever.

The laws of the Lord are true;
    each one is fair.
They are more desirable than gold,
    even the finest gold.
They are sweeter than honey,
    even honey dripping from the comb.
They are a warning to your servant,
    a great reward for those who obey them."
—Ps. 19:7-11

Why is David so in love with God's law? The law and the sanctuary housing it were very near the heart and soul of his passionate relationship with the Lord. People today talk about how important the Ten Commandments are and file lawsuits over the right to display them publicly, yet very few people have them memorized, and I'll bet most of you haven't read them in years! They have become a symbol only. Although they symbolize devotion to God, the statistics we quoted earlier in this book show that our affection for them hasn't done much to change our lives.

I think part of the problem is that the commandments are stated negatively—"thou shalt not" (KJV). I don't know why God gave His commands that way. Maybe for the same reason He appeared in the form of fire—because He needed to make a powerful first impression on the recently freed slaves who were just getting to know Him. All they understood from generations of slavery was harsh taskmasters and cruel treatment. Perhaps that was the only language they understood.

Whatever God's reasoning was and whatever the case may be, we need to look at the law in the light of our society today, taking into account that America prides itself on many things, including the power of positive thinking, and of course endless lectures on building self-esteem. Our culture is much different from that of recently freed slaves. Even that of the time Jesus was here on earth had greatly changed since the Exodus. In Psalm 19 David obviously reinterpreted the law in a positive way, and Jesus Himself turned the emphasis of the law around from negative to positive. In summing up the law He said its intention was for us to love the Lord with all our heart, mind, and soul, and to love our neighbor as ourselves. So let's start out by looking at the first four commandments, which tell us about our relationship with God.

"It was Christ who directed the education of Israel. Concerning the commandments and ordinances of the Lord He said, 'Thou shalt teach them diligently unto thy children, and shalt talk of them when thou sittest in thine house, and when thou walkest by the way, and when thou liest down, and when thou risest up. And thou shalt bind them for a sign upon thine hand, and they shall be as frontlets between thine eyes. And thou shalt write them upon the posts of thy house, and on thy gates' (Deut. 6:7-9, KJV).

"In His own teaching, Jesus showed how this command is to be fulfilled—how the laws and principles of God's kingdom can be so presented as to reveal their beauty and preciousness. When the Lord was training Israel to be the special representatives of Himself, He gave them homes among the hills and valleys. In their home life and their religious service they were brought in constant contact with nature and with the Word of God. So Christ taught His disciples by the lake, on the mountainside, in the fields and groves, where they could look upon the things of nature by which He illustrated His teachings. And as they learned of Christ, they put their knowledge to use by cooperating with Him in His work" (*Christ's Object Lessons* pp. 23, 24).

Chapter 12

The Law and Our Relationship With God

Let's interpret the law through the positive lens of "love the Lord your God with all your heart" (Luke 10:27) that Jesus gave us, beginning with the introductory verse in Exodus 20:2. Once again, the goal of reading Scripture devotionally isn't to master it for its own sake, but to take it into our own hearts and use it to strengthen our relationships with Jesus. This is how I personally pray through the Ten Commandments in my devotional time.

"I am the Lord your God, who rescued you from the land of Egypt, the place of your slavery" (Ex. 20:2).

I always start by thanking the Lord for being my God and for being personal and real and for always being there for me. Then I think through all the things that He has rescued me from. God has saved me more times than I am even aware of. But I remember mostly about my young adult years, when I got lost in the world. I don't know why He has chosen and saved me, but He has, and I will be eternally grateful. Consider all the times that God has saved you. Ask Him to reveal those that you haven't yet noticed. Pray for Him to open your eyes to His leading in your life. We are all slaves to sin and in need of a Savior. This sets the tone for praying through the entire passage.

"You must not have any other God but me" (verse 3). The first commandment makes me stop and evaluate with whom I am spending most of my time. Whom am I most devoted to? I like to pray this regularly in my devotions as a kind of check-in time. What are my priorities? Do I merely say that I'm a Christian, or do my actions prove that it's true?

Is there something you are more devoted to than God? The positive side of this one is to put your emphasis on making God number one in your life. Structure your devotional time. Be intentional about it. Set up your routine and ask God to guide and bless you as you search for Him.

Make Him the one you cry out to both in trouble and joy, just as David did. Learn to talk to Him at all times and in all places.

"You must not make for yourself an idol of any kind or an image of anything in the heavens or on the earth or in the sea. You must not bow down to them or worship them, for I, the Lord your God, am a jealous God who will not tolerate your affection for any other gods. I lay the sins of the parents upon their children; the entire family is affected—even children in the third and fourth generations of those who reject me. But I lavish unfailing love for a thousand generations on those who love me and obey my commands" (verses 4-6).

In ancient times people made literal, physical idols or images. That was part of the culture of the time. They liked to see what they were worshipping. We aren't really tempted to do that today, but we definitely still have idols. Is there a person, possession, or activity you idolize rather than God? The second commandment is really an extension of the first but more specific. People frequently talk about how others "idolize" someone or something. In my devotions I think through my activities and hobbies. Is there something I spend more time doing than I should? Does anything get in the way of my time with God? Many people feel that they just don't have time for devotions because their lives are too busy and hectic. Search for the idols in your life and ask God to help you cut them down and destroy them. Nothing is worth sacrificing your relationship with Him over.

So how do we view this commandment in the positive light that Jesus shed on it? Rather than focusing on tearing down idols—learn to idolize Jesus. Study the Gospels and look at Jesus' actions throughout the Bible. Learn to love Him in the way that David talks about in Psalm 63. Connect with Him devotionally. Make Jesus your all.

Interestingly, this commandment comes with a promise—a promise and a recognition that actions have consequences. It says that sinful idols will have effects that will last for generations. When I think of that, such addictions as alcohol, drugs, and pornography immediately come to mind. Those idols get passed along from parents to children in seemingly endless cycles. Abused children often become abusers themselves, creating unending dysfunction. When you pray through this commandment, ask God to reveal the dysfunctional addictions that you may have grown up with and invite Him to help you break the pattern. Plead for Him to heal you from your past wounds. They can be crippling situations that sap the strength from you and make it hard to connect with God.

The positive side of the promise in this commandment is that when you establish healthy relationships in your family, with other people, and with God, those new patterns will get passed on as well. And God promises at the end of this commandment to lavish unfailing love on you for a thousand generations when you are committed to Him in a loving relationship. When I counsel people with addictions, I advise them to work hard to overcome the addictions—but most of all, focus on filling their lives with God. Sin is difficult to stomp out—it must be crowded out by time spent with God!

"You must not misuse the name of the Lord your God. The Lord will not let you go unpunished if you misuse his name" (verse 7). It is a rampant problem in our society. I regularly hear people taking God's name in vain. I cringe every time someone curses with my Savior's name. Here is definitely one commandment that is helpful in its negative wording: don't do it. But in a society of free speech in which people can bad mouth the president and anyone else, it is easy to do. The best way to overcome the habit if it's a problem for you is to focus on praising God and glorifying His name and all that He is and all that He does. Developing an attitude of praise helps us build respect as well. I have found that most people who take God's name in vain don't know Him. So once again the relationship is the foundation of the cure. Knowing Him builds love for Him, and the result is that we only use His name with respect because of the love.

I have a friend whose supervisor called him into his office one day at work. My friend is someone who openly talked about God and praised Him wherever he was. The supervisor told him to stop talking about God in the workplace because it offended some coworkers. He replied to the supervisor that he would stop using God's name when the coworkers who had complained about him stopped using God's name as well. The supervisor asked what he could possibly mean by that. He said that those who complained about him speaking well of God also employed His name daily —taking it in vain. The supervisor threw up her hands and told him to forget about it and go back to work. Praising God in public is one of the best ways that I know of to be an effective witness!

"Remember to observe the Sabbath day by keeping it holy. You have six days each week for your ordinary work, but the seventh day is a Sabbath day of rest dedicated to the Lord your God. On that day no one in your household may do any work. This includes you, your sons and daughters, your male and female servants, your livestock, and any foreigners living among you. For in six days the Lord made the heavens, the earth, the sea, and everything in them; but on the seventh day he rested. That is why the Lord blessed the Sabbath day and set it apart as holy" (verses 8-11).

The negative way the commandment is stated is definitely the root of some problems we have had with Sabbath observance through the years. We have tended to focus on all the things we don't do and then just end up taking a nap instead of working—getting in our "lay activities." But we need to put the emphasis on the first sentence and on Jesus' positive encouragement to love the Lord your God with all your heart, mind, and soul. To love someone is proactive. You can't love your wife by merely "not" being mean to her. Instead, you must "be" good and "do" loving things in order to stay close to her and have a positive relationship with her. The same thing goes for God. To have a good relationship with Him, we need to spend the Sabbath talking to Him, worshipping Him, learning from His Word, and fellowshipping with the rest of His "body"—the church. We need to do good things together.

I remember one pastor when I was younger who said, "Go ahead and take a nap Sabbath afternoon—but set the alarm!" Don't sleep all day on Sabbath—get a little rest, then spend some quality time with your family and friends in God's presence and in nature if possible. Look over His handiwork, praise His name, and learn to appreciate all that He has made and done for you. It is a holy day set aside to spend time with our holy God and to allow His influence to shape our lives.

Another very important reminder I get from this commandment relates to my daily devotions. When I pray this commandment in my devotional time, it reminds me to take what I like to call "little Sabbaths" throughout the week. I consider my devotional times each day to be breaths of fresh air in my life—like miniature Sabbaths. Just set aside 15 minutes at lunchtime to forget about work and to commune with God. Ask Him for peace and refreshment and wisdom to do your best.

[handwritten margin note: When you have free time, take a mini Sabbath]

This commandment can also refer to bigger events, such as camp meeting and Weeks of Spiritual Emphasis. The Jews had annual Sabbaths, such as the Day of Atonement and the Feast of Unleavened Bread. The more Sabbaths of all shapes and sizes we can structure into our lives, the happier and closer to God we will be. The Sabbath is not a legalistic requirement as much as it's our lifeline to heaven, something to enjoy as often as possible.

I hope you're catching on to the positive side of God's law. I believe that is why David loved it so much—because it kept him close to his God, and he enjoyed the time spent together.

"Christ abiding in the heart shines out in the faces of those who love Him and keep His commandments. Truth is written there. The sweet peace of heaven is revealed. There is expressed a habitual gentleness, a more than human love.

"The leaven of truth works a change in the whole man, making the coarse refined, the rough gentle, the selfish generous. By it the impure are cleansed, washed in the blood of the Lamb. Through its life-giving power it brings all there is of mind and soul and strength into harmony with the divine life" (*Christ's Object Lessons,* p. 102).

Chapter 13

The Law and Our Relationships With People

"Honor your father and mother. Then you will live a long, full life in the land the Lord your God is giving you" (Ex. 20:12).

Finally, a positive commandment! And it comes with a promise for all who keep it, too! Why do you suppose that it is so important to God that we honor our parents? What is honor, anyway? This is how the dictionary on my MacBook defines honor as a verb. And yes, the secular publishers start it off with "we should honor our parents": "*We should honor our parents*: esteem, respect, admire, defer to, look up to; appreciate, value, cherish, adore; reverence, revere, venerate, worship; informal put on a pedestal."

It is easy to honor good parents, isn't it? But this commandment states no conditions. It doesn't say to honor your parents if they deserve it or if you feel like it or if they honor you in return. It merely says to honor them. Maybe it would help if we added "forgive" to that list. I suppose the first place to start practicing forgiveness and reaching out and loving those around us is at home.

We all like to put on a good front in public. It's easier to be nice to people you don't have to live with, isn't it? Some of the most dangerous situations for police to intervene in are situations of domestic violence. Many studies show and many preachers with interests in family matters say that the devil's number one goal is to target the family. If it crumbles, the rest of society goes right along with it. It is the foundation of all that we do and all that we are. As a pastor I know that the three greatest influences in a child's life are home, school, and church. And the school and church pale in comparison to the influence of the family. When we can learn to honor our parents against all odds, we will also be able to honor everyone else we meet on life's journey. The home is the foundation of everything we will know, do, and become. That is why God says that when we honor our parents we will live long, full lives.

"You must not murder" (verse 13). Just four little words. And they sound so easy to keep. Honestly, most of us aren't inclined to go out and physically take another person's life. We could get into the difference between murder and killing, and we could talk about Jesus' teaching that even to hate someone is the same as murder. But you already know that, so I want to go straight to the practical application and how it can have positive effect in our lives.

Rather than "taking life," you must "give life." Not as our Creator breathed life into Adam, but as in helping people to find the happiest and most fulfilling lives possible both on earth and in the next life to come in heaven and on the earth made new. This is the heart of the gospel commission! Yes, living a healthy lifestyle can be a legitimate aspect of the command, but by far the most important is to share the good news of Jesus and His love and what a life committed to a relationship with Him is all about. Leading someone to eternal life in Jesus is the greatest possible gift that we can give to another person and the most rewarding thing we can do.

We can see here how looking at the positive application of each commandment can bring us a dramatically new view of life and take away the tendency to a legalistic religion of self-control and replace it with a loving spirit of self-denial and service to others. That is exactly how Jesus lived out His life on earth in stark contrast to the religious legalism of the scribes and Pharisees of His day.

"You must not commit adultery" (verse 14). Here is another commandment that most people would agree with in its original negative format of "you shall not." Even non-Christian politicians know better than to get caught having an affair—or at least they should. It is one of the most obvious sins, and yet it is one of the most broken rules. Marriage is supposed be a sacred covenant kept "until death do us part."

But the beautiful thing about this commandment is that reversing it in light of "love your neighbor as yourself" turns it into "you shall respect and protect other people—especially women." While the command definitely applies to both sexes, I say "especially women" because they are most often the ones taken advantage of in immoral situations. Most people agree that it is usually men that have the greater sex drive and women give in to it in hopes of being loved or provided for or gaining some other benefit in return. And so the beauty of stating this commandment positively is that it becomes a safeguard against the very thing we are being warned against, not to mention a whole host of other sexual evils, such as pornography, rape, and molestation.

When we look out for and protect the women around us, it helps us to respect and cherish them more and thus makes us far less likely to break the commandment ourselves. Just like the previous commandment, the goal is to promote the well-being of others and allow kindness to rule the day. It goes far beyond sexual sin and includes respect at every level. It is "treat your neighbor as you would like to be treated yourself." As big a problem as this sin is in our society, praying it as a part of a daily devotional routine makes it a constant reminder to fight the battle to overcome the immorality rampant in our society.

"You must not steal" (verse 15). Once again, the way the commandment appears in its negative form is a no-brainer. You can go to jail for stealing, so don't do it. It doesn't make sense. But the positive light that Jesus sheds on it challenges us to give rather than take. Giving is a real challenge for many people in our self-centered society. Materialism encourages us to get as much as we can while Jesus urged the rich young ruler to give everything he had. Jesus knew the danger of clinging to possessions. Sadly, many of us today are walking away, shaking our heads, just as that young man in the Bible did. I'm sure it was a decision that haunted him for the rest of his life.

I remember going to Venezuela several years ago on a mission trip. As we passed through Caracas our guide told us that it was too dangerous to do ministry there. Poverty was rampant in the shantytowns surrounding the city because of high unemployment. Lacking social services, people stole everything they could find and robbed anyone who had something—all in an effort to survive.

The task for us in the developed world today is to find people really in need. It used to be that the churches provided for the widows and the poor, just as Paul talked about in the New Testament. Wherever he went the apostle took up collections for them. But here in America the government assumed that role many years ago, depriving the church of much of its mission. But still the imperative remains to challenge the "me" generations of our world. Jesus Himself said that it is "more blessed to give than to receive" (Acts 20:35).

"You must not testify falsely against your neighbor" (Ex. 20:16). OK, here we go again. This commandment is obvious too. We all know that we should not lie and that one lie leads to another, and when we do prevaricate, we slowly dig a pit that is hard to get out of. Eventually all liars get caught. Once again we have great examples of this in politics, because with great power comes great temptation, and sin follows easily.

Now let's look at the positive side of the commandment. Jesus' interpretation of it through the lens of loving your neighbor as yourself is that rather than saying false things about your neighbor to tear them down, try saying nice things about them and encouraging them! Have you ever had a simple smile from someone passing by brighten your day? How do you feel when someone compliments you? Or when you do it to someone else? As always, do unto others as you would have them do unto you.

People wanted to be around Jesus because He was kind and helpful and encouraging. His stories were simple enough for everyone to understand, and no one felt intimidated by Him. Even merely standing in His presence was an uplifting experience. We have probably all known people whom everyone loves to be around because of their kindness and love. If we could all be that kind of people, our world would be a much better place!

"You must not covet your neighbor's house. You must not covet your neighbor's wife, male or female servant, ox or donkey, or anything else that belongs to your neighbor" (verse 17). We should have the concept by now, so let's go straight into the positive and simple application. Be happy with what you have. Contentment is really a state of mind—a choice. Someone will always have more than you, and there will always be something else that you "need." When Jesus becomes your all, however, it is much easier to be content with what you have. The tenth commandment is really the culmination of them all. Everything in this world dramatically pales when compared with the incomparable Jesus Christ and a loving relationship with Him. He alone—all by Himself—is enough to satisfy the longings of your very soul!

> "Wherewithal shall a young man cleanse his way?
>   by taking heed thereto according to thy word.
> With my whole heart have I sought thee:
>   O let me not wander from thy commandments.
> Thy word have I hid in mine heart,
>   that I might not sin against thee. . . .
> I will meditate in thy precepts,
>   and have respect unto thy ways.
> I will delight myself in thy statutes:
>   I will not forget thy word."
>   —Ps. 119:9-16, KJV

Chapter 14

Using the Twenty-third Psalm to Nurture Our Relationships With God

Psalm 23 is one of the best-loved and most familiar psalms in the Bible, and yet many people have turned it into a vain repetition such as Jesus warned against in Matthew 6:7. It is a vain repetition to most of us in that we can repeat it—oftentimes in unison with others—but we fail to understand it. We will never truly grasp Scripture until we learn to internalize it relationally. The best approach to more fully embracing this passage and more clearly understanding its relational impact is to explore phrase by phrase the meaning of the passage first in David's life and then make application to our own. Since so many people have memorized the psalm from the old King James Version, that is what we will use here.

"The Lord is my shepherd" (Ps. 23:1). At first hearing I suppose many people would consider it a very poetic introduction with all its imagery of the Good Shepherd watching His sheep. It's very idyllic, and many find comfort in the familiarity of it. But the phrase is far more than soothing—it is the very foundation of the Christian life. For David, the Lord truly was his shepherd. He learned to follow His Lord while tending his sheep and composing and singing hymns to Him. The fact that he spent his time preparing such songs and praises indicates that God was constantly on David's mind and heart.

Who of us does this today? What are our minds preoccupied with? How often do we think of our Savior throughout the day? The Scriptures not only contain dozens of psalms written by David about his feelings for his Lord but also record his accomplishments through the power that his relationship with God brought to his life. As a teen he was braver than all the warriors in Israel and the only one so filled with the Spirit that he faced the greatest giant of the day without thinking twice. He went on to show incredible restraint in dealing with the vengeful King Saul. Because of the close relationship he had with God, David refused to plunge ahead in his own power. The relationship is what caused him to be Spirit "filled" and Spirit "led." As a result David became known as a man after God's own heart.

That is why I pray the twenty-third psalm several times per week during my devotional time. Every day I must ask myself if I am allowing the Lord to be my shepherd. It is a choice. We do not have to follow God. So often like sheep we, whether intentionally or unintentionally, stray. Sheep make a choice, and we must as well. It is foundational in my relationship with Jesus to ask myself each morning if I am committed to making Jesus "my" shepherd for the day. Every day the decision is new. As I pray about this, I think through the choices I have been making and ask myself where they are taking me—to the Shepherd or away from Him. My goal is to pray, "Dear Lord, be my shepherd today. Guide my actions and choices and help me to follow You and Your ways." "The Lord is my shepherd" is not a given—it's a choice!

"I shall not want" (verse 1). Here we find the promise that comes with the decision. When David first chose to follow the Lord he still remained a poor shepherd boy for many years. Then he became a fugitive hunted like an animal for even longer. As one intimately committed to God he definitely did not have everything his heart could desire—but he never "wanted" for the basic necessities of life. Through it all David remained faithful to his Lord and eventually became king. Scripture promises that if we are faithful through the difficulties of our own lives as David was in his, we will reign with Christ in heaven (Rev. 20:6) just as David reigned as Christ's anointed king on earth. "I shall not want" is a promise for now and eternity when Jesus is our choice.

"He maketh me to lie down in green pastures: he leadeth me beside the still waters. He restoreth my soul" (verses 2, 3). Part of choosing Jesus as your shepherd is to determine to spend time with Him listening for His voice and observing His ways in nature. Obviously we hear His voice in Scripture—that is why we memorize and dwell on the twenty-third psalm—but we can also personally hear the "still small voice" that Elijah heard so many years ago.

The best way to search for God's voice is to unplug the technology, disengage other people and commitments, and escape to nature. "The heavens declare the glory of God; and the firmament shows His handiwork" (Ps. 19:1, NKJV). Here we can employ the concept of Sabbath that we discussed in the Ten Commandment section. Sabbath is time away from the hustle and bustle of everyday life and commitments. We take a literal Sabbath every week to spend time with God, family, and friends at church, but we also need to take personal Sabbath breaks with God every day. Engaging in devotional practices is a key part of making the most of this time together with Him.

Every morning I take time in a quiet place with God. Sometimes out in nature and sometimes in my office, where I have paintings and photographs of nature scenes. Also I love going to the prayer chapel at my church in which we have a painting of Jesus praying in the garden of Gethsemane. Nature and pictorial reproductions of it will remind us not only of God's love and care for us but also of our Creator's plans for our lives and His desire to live with us forever.

As mentioned previously, I also enjoy spending a half day of prayer monthly in a local Japanese garden where I can listen to the rushing water and see the variety of beautiful plants and trees and the fish in the koi pond while I breathe in the refreshing fragrance of a well-watered garden in full bloom. It is truly nourishing to the soul to sit in such an environment while contemplating Scripture, crying out to God, and listening in turn for His voice. Such times of refreshing are the central part of a devotional life that will help us continually to dwell in His presence and to be filled with His Spirit.

"He leadeth me in the paths of righteousness for His name's sake" (Ps. 23:3). God sent Jonah to Nineveh to tell the people there about Him, because they didn't know their right hand from their left. When we don't know God, we don't know His will, and therefore we don't have any clue about which path to follow either. But when we make Him number one in our lives by spending time with Him regularly, He not only provides for us physically, but gives purpose to our lives as well. Paths of righteousness are the missions that He sends us on because of the desire He gives us to reach out to others both physically and spiritually. Every day as I pray this part of the twenty-third psalm I ask God where He wants me to go and what He wants me to do. As a pastor I have many missions I'm engaged in at any one time, and I ask Him if I'm focusing on His mission rather than my own. Then I pray for guidance on what to do more of and what to turn away from. I ask for His blessing on all my activities, praying that what I do will be a part of His activity in the world. To be working in our own power instead of God's is the surest way to burn out and fail. Jesus wants us to be like the 70 disciples He sent out with His power to preach, heal, and cast out demons. Christ "in you" is the hope of glory—for us and for the world around us (Col. 1:27).

"Yea, though I walk through the valley of the shadow of death, I will fear no evil: for thou art with me; thy rod and thy staff they comfort me" (Ps. 23:4). Hard times will come our way just as surely as they did for David. Not that God wills it, but because of the nature of the devil and his evil desire to destroy us. The great controversy is very real. The question is not if we will ever walk through the valley of the shadow of death, but when and how often. We need to learn to expect and even anticipate trials. Not in a masochistic welcoming of them, but in a preparatory way that reminds us to always be connected to God and filled with His Spirit. Only then can we be victorious in the battle against evil. Just as surely as trials will come, they will also send us down one path or another in the struggle between good and evil. If we are unprepared to meet them, trials can fill us with bitterness towards God and others. But when we are engaged in an active and committed relationship with Jesus, the Lord can use difficulties to help us grown in our dependence on Him and His Word, which will lead to greater peace and joy. Yes, strange as it seems, more trouble can bring more joy! As James said: "Dear brothers and sisters, when troubles come your way, consider it an opportunity for great joy. For you know that when your faith is tested, your endurance has a chance to grow. So let it grow, for when your endurance is fully developed, you will be perfect and complete, needing nothing" (James 1:2-4).

It is a comfort to know that God is always with us in times of trouble, protecting and defending us. And it brings us to the rod and the staff. God has two tools to use as He walks with us through the valley of the shadow of death. The rod is for the enemies. It symbolizes His protective care that doesn't allow us to endure any more than we can handle (1 Cor. 10:13). God employs the rod far more than any of us realize. It won't be until we get to heaven that we will learn of the countless times that He has protected us so well that we didn't even know we were in trouble!

The staff, on the other hand, is for God to use on us. The staff has a hook on the end, and is what a shepherd employs to pull the straying sheep back on the path. He uses it in corrective activity in our lives. Sometimes we have to endure hard lessons before we change our ways. But just as loving parents hate to discipline their children yet know that without it the child's sinful nature will take over their whole lives, so God is willing to use tough love to teach us lessons just as He did when He had to kick

Adam and Eve out of the Garden of Eden to help them learn about the consequences of sin.

As I pray through this portion of the psalm I keep all these things in mind and ask God to guide and protect me through the trials I am in the midst of and the ones I sense coming. I also try to remember to thank Him for the ones He's already seen me through.

"Thou preparest a table before me in the presence of mine enemies: thou anointest my head with oil" (Ps. 23:5). When you are worn out and tired; when you feel as if your prayers aren't getting past the ceiling; when trials have you so beaten down that you wonder if you ever really did have a connection with God—you must remember that God hasn't forgotten about you. While attacks from enemies can be highly distracting and disheartening, keep in mind that Jesus always loves you. Here God promises that one day He will lift you up and prepare a banquet just for you right in the face of those who hate you and plot against you.

Also it is an assurance that if you have enemies you do not face them alone. Jesus Himself had so many enemies that they eventually overcame Him and won the battle against Him—or so it seemed for a while. Saul and others hunted David down like a wild animal for years, and he endured mistreatment and disrespect from his own wife and children at times—yet he was exalted to the position of king of Israel. Jesus was mocked, beaten, and killed—yet He reigns as king of the universe even now. Trials and enemies may pursue and persecute us, but we have the promise that those who choose Jesus as their shepherd will be anointed princes and princesses of His kingdom and will eternally reign with Him (Rev. 20:6)!

"My cup runneth over. Surely goodness and mercy shall follow me all the days of my life: and I will dwell in the house of the Lord for ever" (Ps. 23:5, 6). Keeping this in mind on a daily basis will help us to be constantly aware of our true identity and enable us to act like princes and princesses of God's kingdom in all situations. Then we will approach life with an attitude that allows us to see that our cups are indeed full and running over with blessings, not only here on earth but throughout the ceaseless ages.

If we are to be personally connected with Christ, we must stop using Scripture merely to prove doctrine or read about other people's relationships with Jesus. Instead, we must start employing it as a guide for nurturing our own intimate connection with our Lord. We have seen how the twenty-third psalm invites us to dwell on who the Lord is, to contemplate His loving deeds in the lives of Bible heroes and in our own lives as well.

The invitation of Psalm 23 is to choose and follow the Lord our God and make choices in accordance with His will just as David did. Some days will be good, and others will lead to mistakes, but, like David, we can always recommit and start again. As we bask in the knowledge, experience, and protection that God will provide, we must remember to rest in nature so as to hear His voice and experience His leading. The passage of Scripture we have studied reminds us that we are children of the king of the universe and that He is calling for us to join Him for an eternity of joyful communion, love, and peace. This is what a devotional, scriptural relationship with Jesus can bring to our lives.

> "Listen, O heavens, and I will speak!
>   Hear, O earth, the words that I say!
> Let my teaching fall on you like rain;
>   let my speech settle like dew.
> Let my words fall like rain on tender grass,
>   like gentle showers on young plants.
> I will proclaim the name of the Lord;
>   how glorious is our God!
> He is the Rock; his deeds are perfect.
>   Everything he does is just and fair.
> He is a faithful God who does no wrong;
>   how just and upright he is!"
>   —Deut. 32:1-4

Chapter 15

Witnesses to God's Grace—Add My Name to the List!

The first memorial service I ever spoke at was for my great-uncle Leland. His life was a testimony to me and to many others as well. In the late 1950s he became the farm manager at one of our Adventist colleges out West. In his work he always took care to teach his agriculture students and farm employees how Scripture applied to their trade. Soon after taking over the farm he noticed the problem caused by having students working on Sabbath. Obviously the cows had to be milked, but he still didn't feel right about the fact that the morning crew missed Sabbath school and church. So Uncle Leland started a Sabbath school class specially designed for his milkers to attend when they finished their work. It quickly became so popular that it outgrew the classroom it met in and eventually became known as the "farm church" and later went on to become an established congregation in that college town where he lived and worked. The church still exists today.

Uncle Leland was the son of a faithful Minnesota colporteur and a true man of faith himself. He witnessed his father's faith as a child, learning his ways, and then passed his own knowledge of and experiences with God on to his children and others within his sphere of influence. Leland was a man that was known for reading and rereading many spiritual books, especially his Bible. His family will always remember him as a man of great faith who found his strength and purpose in life while on his knees. My uncle's life was a testimony to those around him, and he challenged and inspired many others to find their own faith as well.

Just before the memorial service I asked to see Uncle Leland's Bible. It was a real privilege to hold in my hands the Scriptures that he read so many times and had practically worn out. Interestingly, the two most underlined passages in his Bible were the Ten Commandments and Hebrews 11. We have already talked about the Ten Commandments in this section. Now I'd like to take some time with Hebrews 11—known as the famous "faith chapter."

Hebrews 11 has greatly influenced many people through the centuries—my great-uncle Leland and those whom he discipled for Christ being just a few of them. Many of them ended up becoming heroes of faith themselves as well. They became heroes because they witnessed both the faith in the lives of the people recorded in the Bible and the faith of those around them. That is how the gospel commission works—we witness the faith of those witnessing to us and then become witnesses ourselves in return. Let's take a moment to discuss how this works.

A witness is someone who sees something and can attest to the fact that it is true. Witnesses can give their version of an accident or crime, or they can relate how they have experienced someone or something. Testimonials are considered the most effective type of advertising, and testimonies at church are often the most convicting type of witnessing, because another person's experience can inspire us to pursue and discover our own. Testimonies put flesh and blood and a face on what a relationship with Jesus looks like.

Witnesses to God's grace naturally give amazing testimonies that are the foundation for effective disciple-making. And keep in mind that our teachings *will* lead to the creation of more disciples if they are true. If our teachings bear no fruit and we reap no results from our efforts, obviously there is a problem somewhere. It shows the importance of having a vibrant spiritual life, because a "changed life" is an infinitely more powerful witness than mere teachings alone. Once again, while teachings are critically important, they cannot stand alone.

That is why Hebrews 11 is so powerful. It is a listing of some amazing accomplishments of people who loved and trusted God and committed their lives to Him in intimate relationships. Let's examine a portion of Hebrews 11 here:

"It was by faith that Abel brought a more acceptable offering to God than Cain did. Abel's offering gave evidence that he was a righteous man, and God showed his approval of his gifts. Although Abel is long dead, he still speaks to us by his example of faith.

"It was by faith that Enoch was taken up to heaven without dying—'he disappeared, because God took him.' For before he was taken up, he was known as a person who pleased God. And it is impossible to please God without faith. Anyone who wants to come to him must believe that God exists and that he rewards those who sincerely seek him.

"It was by faith that Noah built a large boat to save his family from the flood. He obeyed God, who warned him about things that had never happened before. By his faith Noah condemned the rest of the world, and he received the righteousness that comes by faith.

"It was by faith that Abraham obeyed when God called him to leave home and go to another land that God would give him as his inheritance. He went without knowing where he was going. And even when he reached the land God promised him, he lived there by faith—for he was like a foreigner, living in tents. And so did Isaac and Jacob, who inherited the same promise. Abraham was confidently looking forward to a city with eternal foundations, a city designed and built by God.

"It was by faith that even Sarah was able to have a child, though she was barren and was too old. She believed that God would keep his promise. And so a whole nation came from this one man who was as good as dead— a nation with so many people that, like the stars in the sky and the sand on the seashore, there is no way to count them.

"All these people died still believing what God had promised them. They did not receive what was promised, but they saw it all from a distance and welcomed it. They agreed that they were foreigners and nomads here on earth. Obviously people who say such things are looking forward to a country they can call their own. If they had longed for the country they came from, they could have gone back. But they were looking for a better place, a heavenly homeland. That is why God is not ashamed to be called their God, for he has prepared a city for them" (Heb. 11:4-16).

"How much more do I need to say? It would take too long to recount the stories of the faith of Gideon, Barak, Samson, Jephthah, David, Samuel, and all the prophets. By faith these people overthrew kingdoms, ruled with justice, and received what God had promised them. They shut the mouths of lions, quenched the flames of fire, and escaped death by the edge of the sword. Their weakness was turned to strength. They became strong in battle and put whole armies to flight. Women received their loved ones back again from death.

"But others were tortured, refusing to turn from God in order to be set free. They placed their hope in a better life after the resurrection. Some were jeered at, and their backs were cut open with whips. Others were chained in prisons. Some died by stoning, some were sawed in half, and others were killed with the sword. Some went about wearing skins of sheep and goats, destitute and oppressed and mistreated. They were too good for this world, wandering over deserts and mountains, hiding in caves and holes in the ground.

"All these people earned a good reputation because of their faith, yet none of them received all that God had promised. For God had something better in mind for us, so that they would not reach perfection without us" (verses 32-40).

Did you notice that an action always followed the "by faith" statement? And that at the end the heroes of faith will not go to heaven ahead of us? They are waiting to go together with us at Jesus' second coming. We are going to be in some great company on that amazing day!

Check out another famous verse: "Faith comes by hearing, and hearing by the word of God" (Rom. 10:17, NKJV). That is why we must always include the Word of God in our devotions in some way, and then some form of outreach will always be the result.

My favorite part of the faith chapter is the summation that comes immediately afterward in Hebrews 12:1-3. These three verses form another passage that I've prayed four or five times per week for several years. They are some of the most encouraging words the Bible has to offer:

"Therefore, since we are surrounded by such a huge crowd of witnesses to the life of faith, let us strip off every weight that slows us down, especially the sin that so easily trips us up. And let us run with endurance the race God has set before us. We do this by keeping our eyes on Jesus, the champion who initiates and perfects our faith. Because of the joy awaiting him, he endured the cross, disregarding its shame. Now he is seated in the place of honor beside God's throne. Think of all the hostility he endured from sinful people; then you won't become weary and give up."

Always remember that we are not alone in what we go through. Review the lives of the witnesses of old and those from our day as well. Listen to their voices in Scripture and in other spiritual books and stories. They will give you encouragement as you journey through life, one of the reasons that the Bible tells us not to forsake gathering together in church and in other small group meetings. Such witnesses and experiences provide the encouragement that helps us remain faithful and give us the strength to withstand temptation and sin. We must keep our eyes fixed on the prize of living with our Best Friend and Savior, Jesus Christ. After we have listened to the testimonies of those who have gone before, we must then be testimonies ourselves as well.

Wrapping up the Gospel Commission According to Matthew

I hope that you have found some new ways of understanding Scripture in this section—new ways of receiving His Word. If the Word isn't fresh, it won't be refreshing, and if we can't make application to our lives, it's merely academic. God's Word is life-changing when we allow the Spirit to bring it to us in new ways of integrating it into the very way we live. It is only when the Word is fresh and relevant that we will be able to use it to disciple others. People in our world today aren't searching for a new set of rules to follow or dogmas to enforce—they're looking for something to give them love and hope and meaning and power and purpose. They want to make sense of their world and produce a positive difference within it. What most of them do not yet know is that they're looking for what a relationship with Jesus can alone give them. And that is why we need to show them and tell them and teach them how to connect with Him for themselves.

So promise me that you'll never merely skim the Bible disinterestedly again. Whenever you pick it up, remember to find out who wrote or spoke the words you are reading and why. Look at the verses before and after to get the context. Seek to understand what it meant for the people it was originally presented to. Allow the Holy Spirit to deliver the words of Scripture deep into your heart where they can give you life by drawing you close to Jesus. And always ask God to bring biblical principles into your life in a practical way so that you can then share them with whomever God impresses you to in order to bring more and more disciples to Jesus. That is what witnessing is all about. It has changed my life, and I'm sure it will yours as well. By allowing yourself to be witnessed to and discipled by those who have gone before you and then by being a witness to others and entering into discipling relationships with others, you will help lead them to Jesus and thereby be a participant in fulfilling the great gospel commission. Honestly, I have personally found no more rewarding way to live here on Planet Earth.

Part IV

Experiencing His Power

The Gospel Commission According to Mark: Miracles, Signs, and Wonders

"Go into all the world and preach the Good News to everyone. Anyone who believes and is baptized will be saved. But anyone who refuses to believe will be condemned. These miraculous signs will accompany those who believe: They will cast out demons in my name, and they will speak in new languages. They will be able to handle snakes with safety, and if they drink anything poisonous, it won't hurt them. They will be able to place their hands on the sick, and they will be healed" (Mark 16:15-18).

Why don't we expect miracles anymore? Why do supernatural occurrences seem to be so absent from our experience in North America today? Is it possible that miracles are happening all around us and that we are oblivious to them? What are the miracles of our day? In Bible times the miracles of speaking in other languages and protection from snakebites and poison were very important and needed. Lots of people died from simple diseases because they didn't have the modern medical systems we have today, so supernatural healings were their only hope. But our situations have changed today, and God is never stuck in the past—He's always relevant!

Mark's version of the gospel commission promises that when we are filled with the Spirit and engaged in a relationship with Jesus that compels us into all the world to make disciples, miracles *will* follow.

One thing is certain: you don't need miracles to sit on the couch and watch TV or play video games. But when you're committed to your relationship with Jesus, the Spirit and His power will take you off the couch and out of your comfort zone into one in which miracles do indeed abound! In this section we will attempt to discover what kinds of miracles God is performing on a regular basis in our world today and how to participate in them with Him.

Chapter 16

Signs and Wonders in Your Personal Life

Life is hard—even when you choose to give yourself to Jesus. Being filled with the Holy Spirit isn't a magical formula for charmed, effort-free living. Having a meaningful devotional routine and an amazing relationship with Jesus can't ward off all evil. Even understanding Scripture perfectly and enjoying the richness it has to offer can't guarantee that you will always know what to do in the face of challenges. Everyone in the Bible suffered, and so will you. No one is exempt. But it's not your fault. Sure, sometimes we make bad choices and reap the negative results. When you play with fire, you just might get burned! But most of life's problems have nothing to do with you—so don't take it personally. The devil hates us all equally and is bent on the destruction of every thing good that God has created.

In this world we will always encounter trouble. But having a Spirit-filled relationship with Jesus nurtured by Scripture is still the most amazing way to live life successfully—and most of your days will be good and happy, and many will be great and sometimes amazing. But even Jesus, who was perfect, frequently stayed up all night pleading with the Father and crying out to Him. He endured so much stress and anguish in Gethsemane before His arrest and crucifixion that He sweat "great drops of blood" (Luke 22:44). He was whipped and beaten when He had done nothing wrong. In fact, He had done everything good, right, and perfect.

Even though David was a man after God's own heart, he still wrote many psalms wondering why God's presence seemed to have fled and why he felt so alone. But even in our suffering the Holy Spirit is never far away. Romans 8:26-28 says: "The Holy Spirit helps us in our weakness. For example, we don't know what God wants us to pray for. But the Holy Spirit prays for us with groanings that cannot be expressed in words. And the Father who knows all hearts knows what the Spirit is saying, for the Spirit pleads for us believers in harmony with God's own will. And we know that

God causes everything to work together for the good of those who love God and are called according to his purpose for them."

God gave us the Holy Spirit to help us get through life's trials and difficulties. I don't know exactly how the Spirit prays for us with "groanings," but it sounds distressing and painful. Hebrews says that Jesus, as our high priest, is acquainted with our sufferings, and James declares that it is through trials that we learn and grow. If life was pain-free and easy, we wouldn't feel a need for God. And we would never, ever see miracles.

Think about it. Would we need miracles in a perfect world? Did Adam and Eve witness them in the Garden of Eden? And there wouldn't be the promise of signs and wonders in the gospel commission if there was no cosmic battle involved. The truth is that Satan doesn't like God's work and will try everything he can to stop it. But have no fear, God is bigger and mightier than Satan and the end result is sure—Jesus wins!

The key is always to remember that somewhere back behind the scenes God is in control. Eventually the struggle between Him and Satan will end, and the mess we're in will be cleaned up. In the meantime, looking for the miracles along the way can reassure us of God's presence and power and give us relief when we need it most—even when the troubles we face have resulted from our own bad decisions and mistakes. Just as when we looked at Psalm 23 and discussed the valley of the shadow of death, the staff will bring us back on the path when we stray, and the rod will keep the devil and his imps at bay. And both of those activities can happen in miraculous ways!

What Are the Miracles of Our Day?

So if we don't need the supernatural interpretation of other languages, exorcisms for demon-possessed people, protection from snakebites and poisoning, and healing for various diseases that modern medicine can cure as much as people did in the past, what are the miracles of our day? When I want to know how people feel about something important, I ask my friends on Facebook. I think if the "experts" doing research would check in with normal people every now and then, they could give us a lot better answers than they do! A few weeks ago I posted this question in my status bar: "OK—so, I'm almost finished writing my book. But I have a question: What is a miracle?" And here are summaries of a few of the responses from people of all ages, including a student leader from one of my public high school Christian clubs, some retired people, a few church leaders, a guy

I used to party with back in the day, and even a Muslim person seriously thinking about becoming Christian.

"A miracle is something that happens by the direct hand of God. Something that brings Him glory."

"An event that happens by the will of God that is completely unexplainable in human terms and in human thoughts."

"A miracle isn't necessarily a physical healing. It can be a situation or a heart change—meaning that God has a huge variety of things He can do that would be considered miracles :)"

"A miracle is an event that defies human explanation, when the supernatural invades the natural."

"I guess you can say that miracles are the handprints of God in our lives. When He wants to remind us that He exists."

"A miracle is raising a child and realizing how God loves us. When they're toddlers they run around without fear of getting hurt. We try to keep them from going down the slide headfirst. They resist and do it anyway, but eventually they understand why they shouldn't do that. Every child is a miracle. They give us a glimpse of how God feels about us."

"A deistic word for unexplainable positive occurrences."

"Family evening worship as a child when my dad was a literature evangelist—on our knees praying that his sales would be good that week and being thankful for our blessings. Our cupboards were bare. A knock sounded at the door. I went to answer it, and all that was there was a bag stuffed full of groceries! The miracle was that no one knew our situation! My parents were proud people who worked hard and depended on God to provide. I have never forgotten that experience of faith and trust."

"For me it's the result of our faith in God. It's our reward when we humbly come to Him and give Him our all. It's God's almighty power in action."

"We are surrounded by miracles everyday that we don't even see; from the mundane, say texting (think about it), to the sublime—a sunrise; to the amazing—doctors can adjust your heart's pacemaker from anywhere in the world, in real time."

"Everyone is looking for a burning bush, or some other overt 'sign' . . . I read somewhere that coincidence is God's way of choosing to remain anonymous."

"You want miracles? I say look at your spouse, at your garden, right where you are . . . look and see. They're there."

It interests me that no one seems to be expecting to see someone raised from the dead or a blind person healed or another feeding of the 5,000. Jesus doesn't need to perform miracles to "prove" that He is God today—rather, miracles are really intended to show that He cares.

Let me tell you about some of the miracles I've seen in my life.

Ways That God Has Shown Himself to Me
Remember when I told you about when I dove headfirst into the shallow end of a pool, drunk and naked in the wee hours of the morning after a health club Christmas party at the age of 24? how it was a miracle that my neck merely jammed instead of snapping under the weight of my 215 pounds? that it was another miracle that I went on to drive home safely that night without killing anyone, even myself, with my car? Those are what I call defensive miracles and wonders. Defensive miracles are God protecting us from something—including ourselves. On the other hand, offensive signs, wonders, and miracles are God performing miracles as a direct part of the gospel commission to reach other people's hearts or maybe even to reach us. I've experienced lots of those kinds of miracles as well.

I suppose the first time that I ever felt God's miraculous presence was when I was 11 years old. It was at my baptism. An evangelist had come to town to tell us all about God and prophecies and beliefs, and my pastor had been giving baptismal lessons at our little two-room church school in Minnesota as well. At my baptism when I came up out of the water, I felt so pure and holy that I just wanted to go to heaven and be with Jesus right then. That was the most amazing feeling I'd had up to that point in my life, and I knew that God was real because of it. I believe that at that moment Acts 2:38 was fulfilled in my life, and I did receive the promised outpouring of the Holy Spirit in my life.

Sometime after that I lost my sense of connection with God and fell into the routine of church life and doing all the right things. It was more like religion than faith. Then many years later when I was in college and had drifted into the party scene and not long after the drunken mistakes I mentioned above, God gave me a miraculous vision. I can't say exactly how He performed it—I don't remember if it was a dream or a voice or just an impression—but I just knew very clearly that God wanted me to work for Him someday and that I wouldn't always be a drunken fool. I knew He was calling me out of the world and into an amazing life with Him.

The interesting thing is that it happened while I was still entrenched in my worldly ways and trapped in the sins I had chosen. Late one night I was lying in bed, talking with my girlfriend after a night out at the bars and dancing. She was discussing our future and about getting married. Suddenly I told her that I wouldn't always live that way and that someday I would be an evangelist or preacher or something. Rather shocked to say the least, she told me she didn't believe in God and asked if that would be a problem. Yes, I said, it would. We stopped seeing each other shortly after that.

Once I finally left the party world behind God saw fit to put me in a student literature evangelism (LE) summer program. I started selling books for Him only a couple weeks after I had quit drinking. While that whole process was miraculous, let me tell you about the really *big* miracle.

After a year of selling books full-time I was promoted into a leadership position and became responsible for training new students. One evening I was out with one of them for an appointment with a couple interested in some of the children's books we sold. After going through his memorized canvass the student asked the couple which set they were most interested in purchasing for their home. They said they didn't know and asked us to come back. Now, if you've ever worked in sales, that means they will not be getting anything. But the LE work isn't just any sales job. It is a ministry in which you place Spirit-filled publications in homes that then teach people about God and the Bible. The Holy Spirit works with you in this!

When the couple we were showing the books to requested that we come back, the student didn't know how to respond and turned to me—and that's when it happened. The Holy Spirit prompted me to slide off my chair and onto my knees behind the coffee table on which we had displayed the books. At that moment I physically felt the Spirit of God sweep through my body, starting at the tip of my head and flowing down through to my feet. From then on my words literally were not my own. God spoke through me! It was all things that I had said before, but God orchestrated my words and actions in just the right way to impress the couple to purchase the books.

As soon as we wrapped up the sale in that home, the student and I left. We quickly drove to a nearby parking lot where we got out and started jumping with excitement—the student had seen and felt the miracle too! It was the most amazing thing I had experienced to that point in my life, and I will never forget it.

I could tell you about other miracles, such as the time in Nicaragua during a short-term mission trip when God stopped the wind from blowing on the roof of the church we were building (it continued on the ground—just not on the roof) long enough for us to install the metal roof sheeting. If the wind hadn't stopped up there it could have easily whipped the sheeting out of our hands and cut someone very badly. Or I could tell you about the many, many times that I've prayed to God asking what to preach about and within a few minutes I'm running to my office computer to start writing down what the Spirit was impressing me with.

I've seen more miracles in my life than I could list here, but the thing is that many people wouldn't have even noticed them because they happened inside of me—in my heart and mind. God has never used me to heal anyone of a physical malady or raise the dead, and I've never spoken clearly in a language that I didn't know. The miracles I've been a part of mostly revolve around my relationship with God and the little missions He gives me to fulfill and the words He gives me to speak. The really awesome thing is that He wants to do such things in everyone's lives as well, and it *will* happen when we enter into a committed relationship with Him. I bet that if you think hard enough, you can remember a time that God has already done something like this with you. I think they are the best miracles of all.

Chapter 17

Miracle in Peru

I grew up reading stories about missionaries. Now, I'm not old, but when I was a kid the word "Amazon" referred to a river in South America where my favorite mission stories took place. During my childhood "Amazon" was not followed by .com. In order to buy books you had to go physically to a bookstore—as in drive there in your car, get out, and walk in. Searching for books was done by wandering around the store reading signs and book titles unaided by Google. It was kind of like exercise without the gym membership.

Now, growing up in a small town in Minnesota, we didn't have many bookstores—especially not religious ones—so my favorite event every summer was the book sale at camp meeting, where I could get more of the stories about missionaries that I loved to read. We would get the flyer in the mail ahead of time, and I would start poring over it, checking all the books I wanted—it was so exciting! I was one of those kids that would stay up late at night reading with a flashlight under my covers. Since we didn't have a television, reading was the most captivating way to experience other times and places and set your imagination free. Then after reading late into the night I would get up in the morning and go out into the 40-acre swamp on the back part of my grandpa's farm turned junkyard/auto salvage lot and experience my own adventures hacking through the underbrush and shooting at critters with my wrist rocket slingshot all summer (I usually missed). Then my grandpa would hire me to take pot metal off the old Nash and Studebaker cars in his junkyard (if you've never heard of those kinds of cars, Google them). I was Indiana Jones meets Tom Sawyer strangely mixed with Sanford and Son (old sitcom that took place in a junkyard—you can Google that, too).

You should turn off the technology and try old-school reading—as in picking a real book, not something on Kindle or an e-book on your iPad.

I was a graphic design major in college, and I just love the smell, texture, and weight of a new book in my hands as I crack it open for the first time. It took me years to start defacing my precious books with highlighters and pens—I considered them in many ways a work of art. Anyway, after years of reading books about mission adventures and making up my own on the back 40 of grandpa's farm, it was really exciting when I finally had the opportunity to actually go to Peru myself to do mission work along the Amazon river—it was my dream come true.

So I hope you are reading this in old-school book form, but if you do have an electronic version, that's OK too. In fact, if you are close to a computer or iPad, go ahead and check out my Peru mission trip pictures that appear on my Facebook page. I've got some really great shots! And for those of you who Twitter, I started out writing this chapter on the porch of the little Japanese teahouse in the Japanese garden where I like to sit and talk to God. Message me if you'd like to see pictures of it. But now I'm headed to my office, because this chapter needs to be serious, because I'll be preaching about it this week at church.

Anyway, on to the miracle in Peru . . . Before we left on the mission trip I started praying for a miracle (Twitter—I'm sitting in my car in the park parking lot writing this part before driving to the office). Then I wondered what it might be. I kind of wanted to be saved from certain death on the edge of a crumbling cliff on the way to Machu Picchu, or maybe from the jaws of a hungry crocodile after falling off the mission boat I knew we'd be riding in down the Amazon River. But being saved from a rabid monkey with malaria chasing me through the jungle would be a cool story to tell too, or perhaps a giant python would slip into my tent at night, or possibly (Twitter—now I'm writing at 2:00 a.m. because I can't sleep and I'm feeling really creative) the Bora tribe we would be visiting in the jungle weren't really as friendly as people say they are now and might really try to shoot me with poison-tipped blow darts as their ancestors would have—or what if I accidentally tried to force the miracle to happen and it wasn't what God had in mind, and I really died?

I didn't want the miracle to involve anyone kidnapping any of the students going with me, because then other parents might never allow me to take their kids out of the country on another mission trip. Then I got kind of chicken and thought maybe miracles weren't a good idea for this particular mission trip (Twitter—now it's the next day, and I'm in my office at the academy).

But a miracle did happen (if you've been annoyed by all these little Twitter and Facebook interruptions in this chapter, pay careful attention to this paragraph). And here's what it was: We learned how to sit down and talk to people. It was incredibly amazing. When we spoke to a local person from Iquitos, Peru, they were never on their cell phone talking or texting or on Facebook, and they were never gaming or tweeting or surfing either. It was kind of weird. They were never in a hurry to be somewhere else, and they were never running late, because there was nowhere else to be. And they were content with that. Never did they ramble on about the next thing they were going to buy or what they were going to do. They were just there with their full attention on you.

We especially felt strangely close to the kids we met at VBS, even though we couldn't speak the same language. The kids would come up to us—seeking us out. After sitting down with us, they would start talking in Spanish. Then we would answer in English and maybe try some words in Spanish. Although we might not know exactly what each other was saying, somehow we still communicated.

I think we were experiencing a variation on the gift of tongues. Fortunately for us words are only a small portion of communication. It also involves body language, facial expressions and intonation, hugs, perhaps a kiss on the cheek from a child, and laughter—lots of laughter and smiling as well as playing games and chasing each other. And so we turned our cell phones off while we were with them, because we didn't need our phones to make us happy or to entertain us. We learned the joy of really being with the people we were with instead of trying to be with others in lesser ways— such as when you're on Facebook and Twitter while your friends are trying to talk to you. It felt like a miracle. One evening we had an amazing worship with our group as we discussed how it felt actually to be with people in an undistracted way. Truly we were happy there with the children in Peru.

And we felt love in our hearts for the people of Peru. Because of that we left—and will continue to send—parts of our wallets and purses as well. You see, some of the mothers there pleaded with us to help them get uniforms for their children so that they could go to school. School is free in Iquitos, Peru, but you can't go unless you have money to buy a uniform and school supplies. In Iquitos many people still live in thatched-roof homes with floors of dirt or boards. Should you dwell in nearby Belen you may not have walls—just railings and open air. The houses themselves sit up on stilts because of the flooding that swirls around with the sewage from the outhouses as the water rises from the Amazon river. The people there are very poor.

What would your life be like if you couldn't read? How could they consider living in dirt and filth as normal and still be as happy as they were? All of us missionaries carried hand sanitizer in our pockets, and we used it constantly all day long after touching almost anything. Can you imagine giving the gift of education to a child living in these conditions and how it makes the mothers feel when they know their child will get something so valuable, something that they never had?

The poorest person in our missionary group was a millionaire compared to those beautiful, sweet, loving children. But I think we were more blessed than they were by our meeting. They gave us something money cannot buy—the gift of true human communication and tenderness. Those children taught us to sit down and take time to care and to put our priorities in order. As a result, they were and will continue to be miracles in our hearts and lives. To me they will be an enduring memory of how Jesus wants us just to sit down and be with Him every day from now until eternity ends. And the thing about eternity is that it doesn't end. I think heaven will be like being with the people of Peru but in mansions and on streets of gold. Except we won't care about the mansions and the gold—we may not even notice them because they won't be able to compete with the joy of true human fellowship and the wonder of being with Jesus every day, everywhere. That, I believe, will be the best miracle of all.

So, you see, we weren't the first missionaries to this part of Peru, and we didn't need protection from headhunters. Although we had snakebite kits with us in the Amazon jungle, we didn't need miraculous healing for that, either. Nor was anyone trying to poison us. What we needed was to learn to slow down our lives and love God and the people we were with— the Peruvians and each other. If we don't take time for God, we will never learn to hear and follow His voice and share His love with the world. That was the miracle that we needed at that time, and God gave it to us in a powerful way.

Chapter 18

The Miracle of Knowing God

A few months ago God impressed me to have two students from one of my lunchtime campus clubs share their testimonies during one of my sermons at church. In our group we had really been growing in our relationships with Jesus, and these two students in particular were an inspiration to me and to the rest of the group. Here is the testimony of a 15-year-old girl and her relationship with Jesus in her own words:

"Happy Sabbath, everyone! How many of you guys have a best friend? I have several really close friends, and there's no barrier between us. I talk to them about everything—anything that comes to my mind I can tell them. We talk about stuff that goes on at school, any problems with life, clothes, shoes . . . It's just a never-ending conversation with them. And that's my relationship with God.

"God is a best friend. There is no barrier between Him and me. I talk to Him even about things like clothes and shoes. And He listens. We can spend all day talking. It's never-ending. It's continually praying, continually talking. I tell him all my issues, whatever problems I might have had that day, even random things that happened throughout my day that I think are funny. I just tell God, and He laughs with me. When God talks to me, or when I talk to God, I don't feel like I'm talking to someone who's—you know—in heaven. I feel as if I'm talking to someone who's standing two feet away from me. I can hear everything perfectly, clearly. It's just like I'm talking to anyone, any person.

"Now I honestly don't really know how this relationship with God began. Pastor Scott has been urging me to think about how it started, but I really don't know. I never had, as he put it, a turning point. My life has been pretty ordinary, I think, compared to anyone else's. I was raised an Adventist, although I haven't always gone to Adventist schools. But I've had this Seventh-day Adventist belief all my life.

"I remember, though, that last year, my sophomore year, we had a science camp in Albion. One night three other girls and I were sitting in our cabin. It was really late, 3:00 in the morning, and I think we were looking at a magazine or something. But one of the girls brought up how she felt really distant from God. And I remember the rest of us started crying. We were bawling our eyes out for hours. I don't even know how we got through the next day. It was pretty intense. After that day I realized that I needed to get closer to God, so I started writing letters to Him, because I remembered that I could never focus when I prayed to Him. I would start praying and then would think about something else that was going on in my life, and it would eventually get to the point that I forgot that I was praying.

"To focus my relationship I started writing these letters as if it was a diary. I would write them every night, Dear God, blah, blah, blah, whatever. Soon I got really into them. I would even leave the little notebook that I had on my bed faceup so that God could read it. After maybe a month or so I felt really close, and eventually I didn't need to do this anymore. When I would pray to God, I no longer lost my train of thought. Now that I could focus, I stopped writing letters.

"Then early this year around September a few other students and I went to leadership camp. During it we had a Communion service on Friday night. And that Communion service was the first *real* Communion I ever had. Well, I've been in the church all my life and had had Communion before—the bread and the wine—er, uh, grape juice. But that was the first time I ever really experienced it. I remember that we were sitting outside and washing feet with the other fellow students and for the first time really understanding what it was all about. It was no longer a ritual that I did every so often because everyone else in the church was doing it. I had actually understood what it was all about. It was real to me. Well, ever since then my relationship has just gotten better and better.

"I remember God actually was the one who told me to do this (speak in front of the church) against my will. Yeah, I was really forced into this. But anyway, I'm really glad I did now. The thing is—to me—being with God is simple. It doesn't have to be about doctrines or knowing every inch of your Bible. It's just like—I don't know—having Him, feeling His presence there. As good as it is to read your Bible all the time, really, I think prayer is just more of a connection with God. Just talking to Him as you would anyone else in the world. To me, a relationship with God is like a present. But He's more than just the pretty paper on the outside. It's more about what's inside the relationship."

It is a miracle that we, as puny little humans who mess up our lives so frequently, can talk to the God of the universe anytime, anywhere. From a human perspective, it is completely unexplainable. Scientists can't measure or evaluate it. Nor can you bottle it and put it in a museum for everyone to look at. You can only find it in a personal experience that results as you nurture your relationship with God.

The miracle of a relationship with God is always connected to experiences with Him. It's not merely a cognitive understanding. Such things as devotional times and camp meetings become part of our relationships with God and further enhance it. Here is the testimony that another student shared on the same Sabbath as the girl quoted above. He talks about how camp meetings and retreats have affected his life and about a miracle he has seen as a result.

"A couple years ago my mom got really sick. She had headaches that were really bad, but the doctors could not figure out was going on. At first they thought they were migraines, but then they wondered if she had spinal meningitis. They had to hospitalize her. But let me come back to that in a moment.

"How many of you were raised Seventh-day Adventists? All right, nice! How many went to Adventist schools? Cool! What about camp meeting? Anyone go to camp meeting? All right, nice! Well, that's me. I was born and raised Seventh-day Adventist, went to Lodi Elementary and then Lodi Academy. And I have gone to camp meeting every year since I was 4. But even though I did all these really good things, these did not give me a personal relationship with God.

"For me, camp meeting is good for a lot of things. You meet a lot of people—well, mostly girls—but best of all, you experience God without the interruptions of work, school, video games, TV, and just everyday life. I have found that if you just do a normal routine like just go to school and go home and do your homework, you don't have time for God. I see a lot of people, even at school, that just walk around and are sad but don't know why they're sad. I think it's because they are missing something, and I believe that missing piece in their life is God. They're missing a personal relationship with Him.

"Now I've discovered that when I do things out of the ordinary, such as going to leadership camp or Bible retreats, that's when I find God the most. That's when I've felt closer and have a good bond with Him. At camp meeting every year the pastors and stories you hear are just amazing! It makes me feel as if I'm on fire for God. Like I just can't get enough of God and want to get closer and closer to Him. But when I get home it is as if I fall back into my old routine and habits and He just slips away. You just lose it all.

"I have learned that God does not force Himself on us. We have to choose Him. It is our choice. We have to make time for Him every day in our lives. Something that has happened recently to help me strengthen my relationship with God has been a Wednesday lunchtime group at Lodi Academy. We gather in a room, talk about God and our relationships, and—um—just anything, really. Just open conversation, and no one's forced to go. It's just something that happens every Wednesday. At first it started off as a really small group. Four or five maybe. But every week it grows. That makes me really happy. I challenge everyone that goes to Lodi Academy to try it! You don't have to go there every week—just give it a chance. That's my challenge for everyone at Lodi Academy.

"My mom was in the hospital about a week with tests, CAT scans, and MRIs. I was probably the most scared when we were told she had an aneurysm and needed to be transported to the Bay Area for surgery. I remember that my grandpa was at my house, and my mom was in the hospital, and my dad was telling us all this, and we all got really scared. I was in my brother's room, and I remember my dad had to go see her. I said, 'Dad, please don't let Mom die. I love my mom. Please don't let her die.' He looked at me and said he couldn't promise me anything, because it was out of his control. I remember holding my brothers, and we all just sobbed in each other's arms. Then I realized there was only one Person that can help, and that's God.

"So I went to my parents' bedroom, got in their bed, and just cried and pleaded with God to save my mom. Um, I'm not saying it was a miracle, but it really was to me. The next day the doctors revaluated the test results and decided that it wasn't an aneurysm but just a bump in the artery—basically something that had to be watched but nothing serious. It turned out that the cause of the headaches was a spinal fluid leak. So with lots of bed rest and fluids, she healed and didn't need any surgery. God answers prayer!

"This is what gave me a personal relationship with God. If I ever feel distance between God and me, I think back to how He helped my mom and my family. And I know that He is here all the time. If you have a close relationship with God, that's great! But if you don't, God will not force you to choose Him. I encourage everyone to get involved in small groups or reach out to a friend or pastor or someone that can help you get into a day-to-day routine to make God a part of your everyday life."

Is it all starting to come together for you? Our view of God, how we read the Bible, how we interact with the Lord personally and corporately, and the power and miracles that He brings to our life all together form the heart and soul of Christianity. But we all experience it differently. Some people have their faith sparked by a miracle, while for others it seems as if it's just always been there. Later we will get into the structure of devotional life a little more and explore how to engage different spiritual opportunities that will help us live our spiritual lives to the fullest. Life with God is simple, but there are things that need to be scheduled and orchestrated to make it the rich life that He wants it to be. Discipline is key.

Our devotional life is the foundation from which miracles spring forth. We must invite God into our lives so that He can fill them with His Spirit. Then He can flow out from us into the world around us. So far we have looked mostly at the miracle of God's presence in the personal life. But what about the old-fashioned miracles such as you read about in the Bible times? Are they still happening out there somewhere?

Chapter 19

Old-School Miracles: God's Power Unleashed!

Can you imagine what it must have been like to be one of the children of Israel leaving Egypt? You're packing your stuff in the middle of the night to flee your life of slavery. In the weeks past you've witnessed plagues of flies and frogs sweep across the land, invading every aspect of life. The mighty Nile River has turned to blood, cattle have been wiped out, and the firstborn son of every home not committed to God has perished. Tragedy after tragedy has wreaked havoc in Egyptian society, yet your own small place within that world has remained safe through the mighty hand of God. His hand can unleash positive miracles and negative ones as well. It's hard to understand, but it happens all throughout the Old Testament of the Bible. The Lord gives, and He takes away. I don't know that we can ever understand it, but it is what it is. God is God, and we are not.

What must the Israelites have felt as they left their lifelong homes in the middle of the night, only to head straight into a dead end at the Red Sea? Trapped and facing certain punishment and possible death, they cried out to a God that many of them had just met for the first time, and He answered in the most miraculous of ways. Many of those former slaves may have never even seen a sea before. I wonder how they felt when they saw something split the water and pile it up on either side, opening a dry path ahead of them. It was a miracle for people with a very new and weak faith. God performed His miracles to get their attention and build a foundation for their faith.

The Lord could have struck down the Egyptian army's horses as they pursued the Israelites as he had already done the cattle. He could have inflicted blisters on the Egyptian soldiers' feet to stop them from marching just as He had sent boils all over their bodies only a short time before. That's how all the other miracles had gone—why was it different this time? Why did God permit His chosen people to come under attack instead of allowing them to continue being bystanders as they had before, when they watched miracles unfold around them while they sat protected in their homes? Why did God split the sea and make them cross in fear that the water may come crashing down on them instead of letting them walk on water like Peter, or why didn't He let them fly across on chariots like Elijah?

I don't really have any good answers to such questions. Nobody knows, so all we can do is speculate. I do, however, think that one thing is for sure. God wanted the Israelites to own their faith. Hearing stories of great miracles in the past is really cool. Incredible answers to prayer can be inspiring—that's why we read the Bible and share testimonies. But the bottom line at the end of the day is that the faith of our fathers cannot be a substitute for our own faith. Faith in God demands an experience with Him—a personal experience that each individual can only find for himself or herself. That may be why God took the Israelites from being bystanders watching the miracles happen around them to actually being in the midst of the storm and needing the miracles themselves. Today, we need to be in the midst of miracles ourselves as well, in order to fully experience God for whom He is, and that is why He is still in the business of creating miracles. Check out this modern-day miracle story that I got from a friend who used to travel the world with an organization that spent their time making videos about missionaries working with remote tribes in developing countries.

"It was about 8:00 a.m., and we were just getting ready to leave for a three-day boat trip out of the jungle. A group from the school in Guayaramerin had been helping us for the past two weeks for their school mission trip. Just then a young man came to the house asking if I would check on his pregnant wife. Her water had broken. She was a 16-year-old girl, seven months along. We strongly encouraged them to go to the next village to radio for a plane. From there it would only require 30 minutes to get to the hospital by plane. But it would take three days by boat with us, so we urged them to travel by plane if possible. Furthermore, we didn't even have a radio to communicate for help if a problem arose. All I could do was cry to the Lord for help. We just prayed and encouraged the couple to do what they thought would be best for the baby. I had always dreamed of being a missionary nurse to help deliver babies while working for the Lord, but now my dream had turned into a nightmare.

"When we had finished loading the boat, the young couple came to join us. My heart sank as I thought of all the things that could happen during the next three days. I had spoken with other missionaries, and we had prepared all the medical equipment that we thought we would need for a delivery. During the first day of the trip the couple was calm. They spent their time visiting with the students and even asked one of the students, who had a Bible, to study with them. That night we camped at a village and started off early the next morning. Everything was well with the mother-to-be. Her vitals were stable, and she denied any pain or discomfort. As we traveled along the river I continued to pray that we would arrive at the city in time. Just before lunchtime, I noticed the young wife make her hand into a fist. I knew she was in terrible pain. When I asked her when the pain had started, she said sometime in the morning. 'Why did you not tell me?' I asked her. All she could say was that she was afraid, and now I was afraid as well. I hadn't delivered a baby since I gave birth to my own daughter 11 years earlier!

"A speedboat happened to be passing by. Jumping to my feet, I started yelling, knowing that at times ADRA travels the river with doctors. When the boat turned around, to my disappointment it was not full of doctors as I had hoped, but instead a bunch of intoxicated men staring back at us. We explained the situation, and they said they would be back down our way in an hour or so. All my hopes sank as their boat roared away.

"Springing into action, we made the young pregnant woman as comfortable as we possibly could. We hung a cloth up to divide the boat to give her some privacy. Her contractions were now coming hard and fast. A few of the students helped with her vitals and an IV drip, while another had elevated her feet, hoping it would help slow down the labor, but nothing worked. As the contractions continued, everything indicated that it would be a breech delivery. Fully aware of the dangers of the medical situation, my heart cried out to the Lord for guidance. Things had become serious. The baby's legs and bottom were out but the head would not pass through. All the procedures I could remember had no effect. I realized during this crisis that a greater battle was going on behind the scenes. The enemy did not want the Lord to be honored or glorified. Here with us, witnessing everything, we had villagers and students waiting to see the power of their prayers. It could be a living testimony of God's power. I cried out to the Lord for help, and He answered. *You must do an episiotomy.*

"*Lord, I have no anesthesia,* I replied in my mind, *but, yes, Lord, Your will be done.* Within a few minutes we had the baby out, but when I turned the little form over, my heart sank. She was blue and lifeless. Within an instant Mindy, one of the student helpers, saw a small heartbeat inside the little chest. Quickly we performed CPR, and within no time at all she started to turn pink and took her first breath.

"Just as we were finishing the delivery and helping the new family member, to my surprise the speedboat had returned and offered to take us to the nearest town. So with our homemade bed for the mom and baby, another missionary and I went rushing away. Within two hours we had reached the next town. If we had stayed on our boat, it would have taken us another day and a half to arrive at the same town. The baby had continued to struggle as we traveled, but she was holding her own. As soon as we reached the town, I ran into the hospital, calling for help. The doctor came out and looked down at her small, frail body and said she was gone. Then as if to say 'No, I will *not* die,' she gasped for air. The doctor took her into the hospital and gave her the care she needed. While I watched them save this little life the presence of the Lord filled my heart to let me know that in each of us is a child that He is saving.

"We ask as you have read this story to keep us uplifted in prayer. Please pray for the Lord to continue to direct our work on the river and for more missionaries who would desire to live and work in the villages" (Cornelio and Susan Moro, *Miracle on the River,* Guayaramerin, Bolivia).

Yes, the Lord is still a God of wonders and miracle-working power. Events take place every day that can only be explained as divine intervention. Miracles today are not uncommon. If you search the Web and bookstores, you can still find incredible stories happening out there. Many of you may have seen the movie *Faith Like Potatoes* or heard of other miraculous accounts.

But what about the really huge miracles, such as those performed in Egypt? Why aren't we seeing ones of that caliber today? Until God sent Moses and Aaron to Pharaoh to demonstrate God's power, the Bible does not record many between then and the miraculous birth of Isaac.

Then after God delivered the chosen people from slavery and established them in their land, the prophets primarily focused on messages to repent and return to God and a committed relationship with Him. For the most part such messages did not come with miraculous signs and wonders. Those times were much like ours today—the miracles were smaller and more personal.

Thus it seems that miracles in the Old Testament varied in greater or lesser number and degree as needed during different periods. Some of the times of greater miracles were even prophesied beforehand—two of them symbolized as the early and latter rains. The early rain referred to the time the Christian church would be established at Pentecost after Jesus' ascension, and the latter rain, the time God would unleash the greatest power, would be the period just before Jesus' second coming. At that time supernatural power will help God's people deliver the gospel message powerfully to the world one last time.

Notice that the Old Testament records the most miracles at Creation, the Flood, and the Exodus. And notice that all the miraculous activity in the Bible is intimately connected to God establishing and preserving our relationships with Him—miracles to draw His people to Him and to protect His people from those who would destroy them. Then the Old Testament predicted that in the future even greater supernatural activity would occur again about the first and second comings of Christ. Notice that it all revolves around Jesus and points us to Him—our Creator, Deliverer, Example, and Savior.

We are seeing comparatively fewer miracles right now because it is the metaphorical winter—the time between the rains. But winter has been going on for a long time and must be reaching an end. The storm clouds are gathering, and the latter rain will pour down soon.

Chapter 20

Preparing for the Latter Rain

So where does the imagery of the early and latter rain come from and what does it mean? I live in California's Central Valley, and our climate is in many ways rather similar to that of Palestine in Jesus' day. We grow many of the foods that Jesus talked about in His parables and stories: wheat, grapes, olives, figs, etc. Here in the Central Valley it rains in the winter but not in the summer. Typically the showers start in September or October (like the early rain) and then end in April or May (like the latter rain).

In Israel, since they didn't have irrigation, it meant that they grew many of their crops in the winter—planting in the fall and harvesting in the spring. The early rain was important because it prepared the ground for sowing and got the plants off to a growing start, and the latter rain in the spring was the last extra push to help the crops fill out and mature. A good latter rain was important for a good crop. Here is what the Bible says about the early and latter rains:

"And it shall be that if you earnestly obey My commandments which I command you today, to love the Lord your God and serve Him with all your heart and with all your soul, then I will give you the rain for your land in its season, the early rain and the latter rain, that you may gather in your grain, your new wine, and your oil" (Deut. 11:13, 14, NKJV).

Now today in California we have irrigation to make our crops grow exactly as we want. But in Bible times they had to depend on the rains to survive. If the rains did not come, there would be no crops, and the people would be hungry and eventually starve. The Bible talks about a devastating famine caused by the lack of rain in Elijah's day. In that instance, God withheld the rain, because the people had strayed from Him and worshipped idols. He prevented the rain until He finally got their attention. That is also why the children of Israel moved to Egypt and were eventually enslaved there—because of famine in the land caused by a lack of rain. Rain meant life—no rain meant death.

The imagery of the early and latter rains as used in the Bible symbolizes spiritual life and death. The spiritual rains refer to the outpouring of the Holy Spirit that fills those connected to God and inspires them to share their testimony of their experiences with Him. As a result, it wins even more hearts for Jesus and produces an even greater spiritual harvest. By looking at the early rain that fell at Pentecost we can start to get an idea of what the latter rain may resemble and what it may mean.

First of all, the latter rain is going to be amazing! Have you ever tried to imagine what the early rain looked like at Pentecost? The book of Acts says that the disciples prayed for days in an upper room, pleading for the promised outpouring of God's Spirit, and then it came falling down upon them in the form of tongues of fire. The sound of a mighty rushing wind accompanied it as it happened, and then the miracles started when people spoke in various languages all at once so that everyone could understand. It converted 3,000 people in a single day.

The early followers of Jesus obviously had great relationships with Him that they had formed while He walked with them here on earth—they were totally committed to Him just as David was and just as we are to be. Their relationships with Him were the foundation of the power they received from Him.

The promise of the latter rain declares that people will still have intimate and personal relationships with Jesus just before He returns to earth, and it will be through those relationships that God will work His miraculous wonders in that day. That is why today's miracles are primarily taking place in the hearts of God's people—He is trying to draw us close to Him in preparation for the latter rain and His subsequent soon return. His desire is to prepare us now for the miraculous manifestations of His power and glory that will soon burst forth in our world.

Have you ever wondered what those miracles of the last day and the latter rain will look like? What is it that our world would respond to today? We have so many amazing special effects from Hollywood that we see on the big screen and the miracles of modern medicine and digital technologies and engineering as well as the "shock and awe" of our modern military that it seems nothing new could surprise people today. Revelation 13:13 states that the devil can perform "astounding miracles, even making fire flash down to earth from the sky" in the sight of humanity. What could

God do that would be even more impressive than all this? It's hard for us to imagine, but Scripture promises that God's latter rain will indeed be more powerful than anything else for drawing humanity to Him. I don't have any idea what the drama will all be about, but I do know that somewhere within it all—in the midst of the fire and earthquakes and windstorms—the still small voice of God will continue to call to us and to the world as it did to Elijah.

If the miracle of knowing Jesus intensifies near the end—and I believe it will—incredible events and natural disasters may happen that will turn people's hearts toward Him as they search for answers to their deepest desires. Maybe some of the miracles will be to somehow make the pleasures and technologies of this world grow weak and stale in the light of Jesus and eternity with Him, because our world, while it excels in providing excitement, is seemingly incapable of bringing peace.

Jesus may be drawing you into a closer relationship with Him now, because that is the area in which people will come seeking guidance from you. Maybe they will start asking you about Him at work. Perhaps a lunchtime Bible study and testimony session will spontaneously spring forth. I believe that the truest form of evangelism is when one person shares their spiritual experiences with another—building and strengthening the true bonds of brotherhood and sisterhood. I believe the stories of Acts 2 and 3 can happen again, because that is the essence of the gospel commission—Jesus giving Himself for us, and we giving ourselves for each other.

It just may be that in the last days the miracles that people will be asking for will not be for physical healings such as Paul and Peter performed through God's power in the book of Acts. Rather, it may be that the focus will be on the miracles of peace and tranquillity through a personal relationship with Jesus that will be most prized in our overcrowded and hurried individualistic world. People today have to go to counselors to find a listening ear and a comforting voice. Others take drugs and use alcohol and each other's bodies to try to calm their shattered nerves and satisfy their misplaced desires. It seems that the more technology and entertainment advances, the more peace retreats—just as my mission group and I discovered in Peru.

I cannot fully imagine what the offensive and defensive miracles of that day may be that will drive us to our knees, seeking Him in the midst of the great controversy, but I do know that the evidence the Bible provides shows that God performs all miracles not to satisfy our selfish desires, but to draw us closer to the One who loves us more than life itself—the One who proved that love by giving His all for us upon the cross. The miracle of Jesus in our lives is the answer to every question, and a relationship with Him is how those answers reach our hearts.

An interesting prophecy in the book of Joel talks about some of the miracles that will happen at the end of time:

> "Then, after doing all those things,
> I will pour out my Spirit upon all people.
> Your sons and daughters will prophesy.
> Your old men will dream dreams,
> and your young men will see visions.
> In those days I will pour out my Spirit
> even on servants—men and women alike.
> And I will cause wonders in the heavens and
> on the earth—
> blood and fire and columns of smoke.
> The sun will become dark,
> and the moon will turn blood red
> before that great and terrible day of the Lord arrives.
> But everyone who calls on the name of the Lord
> will be saved."
> —Joel 2:28-32

Doesn't that sound amazing and maybe a bit confusing too? People prophesying and receiving miraculous visions and supernatural occurrences happening in nature? Acts 2:17-21 quotes this prophecy during the time of Pentecost and the early rain, in which it was actually fulfilled! Did you know that the Bible records the fulfillment of lots of prophecies? They serve as actual proofs that the prophecies were true. But according to Scripture a second fulfillment of this prophecy in Joel is still to come. The context of the original prophecy (Joel 2:23, 24) indicates such a second fulfillment:

> "Rejoice, you people of Jerusalem!
> Rejoice in the Lord your God!
> For the rain he sends demonstrates his
> faithfulness.

Once more the autumn rains will come,
as well as the rains of spring.
The threshing floors will again be piled high
with grain,
and the presses will overflow with new wine
and olive oil"

The autumn and spring rains mentioned here are translated as the "early" and "latter" rains in other versions of the Bible. The early rain refers to Pentecost that has already been fulfilled, and the latter rain points to the approaching time just before Jesus' second coming. Notice how the prophecy ends in the first passage we quoted. It says those things will happen "before that great and terrible day of the Lord arrives. But everyone who calls on the name of the Lord will be saved" (verses 31, 32). Here we encounter the second fulfillment, or the prophecy of the latter rain. So once again, when the book of Acts cites the passage, it has only the first fulfillment in mind. The latter and greater fulfillment will take place just before the day of the Lord, which is the Second Coming. James 5:7 also speaks about this second fulfillment when it too mentions the latter rain in the context of Jesus' return.

Now, I'm not a prophecy expert, and I don't like getting into technicalities, but I believe that it is critically important to try to understand at least the basics. And that is we need to be found in the upper room praying for the Holy Spirit and fellowshipping with other believers in the Spirit just as Jesus' followers were at the time of the early rain in Acts 1. The Spirit will be poured out again in even greater measure than at Pentecost at the time of the latter rain, and I believe it will be happening far sooner than we think.

Pulling It All Together and Wrapping It Up!

Let's see if we can summarize the first four parts of this book in a way that makes sense. In the first part we considered how the entire Bible is the story of God searching for us and desiring personal relationships with us. We also touched upon David's passionate pursuit of God. In addition, we studied how to nurture our own relationship with God on a daily basis by using all of our senses to connect with Him just like the examples we found in the Old Testament sanctuary.

In the second part the supernatural world is real and very powerful.

We find the dark side and all its enticements constantly portrayed in the media that surround us—movies, books, and music just to name a few. But no matter how fascinating the world makes such things seem, the Bible tells us clearly that they are a sure path to destruction. Jesus, on the other hand, is even more mysterious and powerful in His love, power, and majesty as we discovered in Psalm 18, which pictures Jesus thundering down from heaven on an angelic being to save David from his enemies, and also in Ezekiel 1, in which we find a mind-boggling description of what angels really look like. In the end it is God's love that overpowers every other force—no matter how evil—in the universe.

Then in the third part we examined several passages of Scripture to learn how to read the Bible devotionally—in a way that can nurture our relationship with God rather than just dig out information about Him. We looked at such familiar passages as the Ten Commandments and Psalm 23 in new and compelling devotional ways.

Finally, in the fourth part we explored the miraculous lives that God promises we will all experience when we are committed to a daily relationship with Him. Today God's power is busy working in the hearts of all His people, preparing them for the end of the world and the mighty miraculous manifestations that will accompany it.

We can summarize this all in several vital questions: Do we understand God for whom He really is? Are we receiving His Word? Are we getting to know Him personally? Are we experiencing His power? These first four parts sought to help you understand how to know Jesus better and how to live for Him. Now, we will turn to the fifth part, in which you will find some practical, implementable tools to use in actually developing your own personal relationship with this mighty, awesome, and loving God that we've been talking about.

"We proclaim to you the one who existed from the beginning, whom we have heard and seen. We saw him with our own eyes and touched him with our own hands. He is the Word of life. This one who is life itself was revealed to us, and we have seen him. And now we testify and proclaim to you that he is the one who is eternal life. He was with the Father, and then he was revealed to us. We proclaim to you what we ourselves have actually seen and heard so that you may have fellowship with us. And our fellowship is with the Father and with his Son, Jesus Christ. We are writing these things so that you may fully share our joy" (1 John 1:1-4).

Part V

Living Life Devotionally

Taking Action:
Establishing Your Own Testimony

We have come to the point at which belief must lead to action. You begin to develop your own testimony, because now you experience God in a way that you just can't keep to yourself.

No matter how wonderful and compelling the ideas of the previous chapters may sound to you, if you don't start "doing it," nothing in your life will change. If you don't take action, you'll still be living in your own power instead of God's, and you'll keep on making the same old mistakes and suffering the same old consequences.

On the other hand, when you learn to live life with Jesus every day, you will experience victory and joy and happiness such as you've never known. You will be able to sing of Jesus' love as David did in Psalms, and it will be easier to be patient and to love others. Life will be far more satisfying, and you'll handle its trials and tribulations of life with a strength not your own. As a result, you'll see miracles around you that you've never noticed before and will begin to sense the spiritual world battling behind the scenes of the great controversy.

So dig in, do the work, and experience the joy. Just like your marriage, career, or health, you get out of your devotional life what you put into it—except that with the devotional life you get to experience not only a great relationship with Jesus by committing yourself to Him but also a better marriage, a more successful career, and better health, as well as more success in all your relationships and endeavors. A healthy relationship with Jesus is the foundation of a well-lived life.

Check out the structure, try the four-week daily devotional guide and journaling, look over the tools in chapter 26, and then set up your own customized devotional routine for living your life with Jesus.

Chapter 21

The Structure for Living Life Devotionally

Relationships are fluid, having a natural ebb and flow and spontaneity that can be lots of fun. But they also need to have structure. When two people are dating, the relationship is often free-flowing and exciting. But when marriage sets in, at some point you have to intentionally set up date night and laundry schedules and shopping lists and eventually routines for the kids, or it all falls apart. That's how it is with our relationships with Jesus, too.

People frequently give their lives to God after a life-changing, emotional experience, but then, when the newness wears off, they don't know how to maintain the relationship, and it slowly fades or even dies. Our devotional lives need structure, just as our marriages and other relationships do. That is why Jesus created the weekly Sabbath right after He created Adam and Eve themselves—He knew they would need it.

God also went on to establish annual festivals to remind the children of Israel of His leading and miracles in their past. Then both in Jesus' day and throughout much of the Bible there were set prayer times throughout the day to remind the people to spend time talking with God and remembering His words. Let's take some time to develop our understanding of how a devotional structure can help guide you into the life with Jesus that you really want to live. You will notice that the activities listed below include both personal and corporate activities. We all need individual devotional time with Jesus as well as time together with other believers.

Annual Events for the Big Recharge

Going from big to small, we'll start out with the major events that can recharge your spiritual life and give you a boost at scheduled times throughout the year:

Christmas is the most obvious place to start. It happens every year—in a big way—and you can't miss it. Put Jesus back in the holiday as you never have before. Read the Christmas story with your family a few verses at a time during the weeks leading up to the special day. Downplay the commercialism. Talk to your family and pray about what you think God would like you to do differently to put the emphasis on others instead of just yourselves. Maybe you'll decide to give each other one gift less so that you can help a family in need. Be creative in making Christmas the most spiritual holiday of the year.

Camp meetings and spiritual retreats are important for bringing revival to your life as well. Look over your conference Web site for women's retreats, men's retreats, camp meeting schedules, and evangelistic meetings. Mark your calendar now and book your reservation today. No matter how you might feel at the moment, you will be glad when you are there. Oftentimes we don't realize how spiritually dry we are until we are revived. So schedule it now, and you'll be grateful later.

Monthly/Weekly Events for a Spiritual Shot in the Arm

I participate in several monthly events to give my spiritual life a boost as well. The most foundational for me is an extended time of prayer. I referred to this earlier in this book when I talked about going to a little Japanese garden in a park just outside of town. Usually ending up being two or three hours and incredibly refreshing, it helps me to stand back and take a look at my relationship with Jesus and get a fresh perspective on where I am spiritually. As a pastor I can put it into my schedule on a weekday morning, but for most people a Sabbath afternoon or Sunday morning may work better. Such special time lets us forget the world and just walk and talk with Jesus, allowing Him to bring rest and regeneration to our lives and souls.

Christian fellowship is important as well. I attend a monthly area Adventist pastors' network as well as a monthly youth pastors' organization that involves youth pastors of all denominations in my area. Both are good for encouragement and to get a perspective on what the areas of need may be where I live.

I also recommend joining a small-group fellowship/Bible study. Our church has a strong small-group ministry that is a tremendous blessing to those members who participate. Ask your pastor and church secretary about opportunities in your area. Also check the Internet for groups such as Moms in Touch, in which mothers gather together weekly to pray for their local public schools and the teachers, students, and Christian clubs on campus.

Finally, don't forget about Sabbath school and church. I would like to challenge you to rethink why you attend those services each week. For many people Sabbath school and church are merely a social tradition that makes them feel as if they've completed their religious duty for the week. Others expect it to be the one time they get spiritually "fed" for the week. With this mind-set many people are putting the responsibility for their spiritual lives on someone else's shoulders instead of their own. As a result they often make various complaints about church, such as "It's boring" or "The music isn't my style" or "There are too many hypocrites."

The beautiful thing about having a vibrant devotional life is that it helps to change your attitude toward church from that of being a consumer to that of becoming a contributor. When you are feeding yourself spiritu-ally every day, you can then go to church with more of an attitude to wor-ship God, share testimonies, and encourage others rather than expecting the church to "meet your needs." Devotional living is far healthier spiritu-ally for both you and for your church. And it is how God intended for the body of believers to function.

Your Personal Weekly Devotional Time

Now, let's look at the weekly cycle for your daily personal devotional time. To do that we need to understand our personal spiritual needs as they fluctuate from the beginning of the week, to the midweek recharge, and to preparing for Sabbath. It is just the basic overview of what most people need throughout the week. We will get into the specifics of daily devotions in the next part.

SABBATH: THE HEART OF THE DEVOTIONAL LIFE. God created the Sab-bath to be the foundation of your life with Him. Sabbath school and church are indispensable for recharging your spiritual batteries. Then after some lunchtime fellowship and some afternoon hours in nature or with family, the early evening is a great opportunity to establish your devotional em-phasis for the week. Sabbath is the perfect time to decide what passages of Scripture you will focus on during the week to come. You may decide to base your passages on the sermon you just heard or on the same topic as the Sabbath school lesson, or you may select something completely differ-ent depending on where you feel you are spiritually and where you want to go (see chapter 26 for an overview of the Bible and guidelines for deciding which passages of Scripture to choose).

SUNDAY: A RUNNING START FOR THE WEEK. On Sunday you can get your devotions started for the week based on what you set up for yourself on Sabbath. Perhaps you can do some fine-tuning on where you want to go and maybe even take a little extra devotional time to get yourself off to a good start.

MONDAY: HELP FOR THE MONDAY MORNING BLUES. Today you will really be grateful that you have set up your devotions for the week. When Monday morning hits and the grind begins, it can throw your whole devotional routine off track unless you are well organized and ready. If need be, you can even have part of your devotional time in your car if you have a freeway commute of 15 minutes or more. I have often sung and recited Scripture in my car on the way to meetings out of town. If you are a regular traveler, make your car a sanctuary in which you regularly meet with God.

TUESDAY: REACHING OUT AT WORK. On Tuesdays most people start settling into the weekly routine—both spiritually and with work or school. It is a great day to start sharing what you are learning in your devotions or what God is doing in your life. I know of many people who are a spiritual breath of fresh air in the workplace. Remember—what you don't use, you'll lose. If you don't exercise your faith by sharing it, you can become spiritually gluttonous and end up in spiritual cardiac arrest.

WEDNESDAY: THE MIDWEEK RECHARGE. Prayer meetings and small groups have typically met midweek because we need a spiritual boost by Wednesday. A midweek meeting not only nurtures your Christian fellowship needs but it can also enhance your personal devotional time as well and get you back up and running for the final push through to the end of the week. Even if you aren't feeling weak spiritually, it is important to increase your strength before you do. Wednesday is often the day that devotional times begin to crash for the week, so always remember that prevention is the best medicine for the spiritual blues!

THURSDAY: FINISHING STRONG. If you can make it through Wednesday and get a recharge then, it will help you to be back on top again for some more outreach and sharing on Thursday. As you realize the week is almost over you can think back over it and celebrate the spiritual victories and examine the areas of weakness that you'd like to work on. Pray for opportunities to be a witness so that you will have a fresh testimony to share when Sabbath comes.

FRIDAY: HERE COMES THE SABBATH! For many Adventists Friday means getting off school or work at noon to prepare for the Sabbath. This adds for a little variety to your life as you take an early break from work to prepare your home and yourself for a special Sabbath day with Jesus that begins on Friday night! This is the blessed rest that our Savior knew we would need even before sin entered our world.

The Daily Routine

Remember why Daniel was thrown into the lions' den? Because everyone knew about his set prayer times. Throughout much of the Bible era faithful Jews turned at morning, noon, and night toward the Temple and prayed. Many people have found set devotional times to be a good practice still today. Here are some suggestions and ideas for your daily prayer times that have worked for many others as well as for me, and they may help you as well.

MORNING: GETTING STARTED RIGHT. For me, it is typically the longest of my daily devotional times—normally about 30 minutes. I often like to start my morning devotional time with a few minutes of silence just to relax and forget about whatever I may be facing that day—I try to focus solely on God. Other times I like to begin by singing or listening to Christian music, while on still other days I may dive right into my prayer time if something specific is on my mind, or then again, I may head straight into Scripture. Every day can be different as you learn to get a feel for your devotional life and your spiritual needs.

As mentioned in chapter 4, I may light some incense to remind me of the sanctuary symbols and their meaning, and I may bring back some memories of Friday nights as a child or the Christmas story. Other days I may brew some herbal tea and enjoy the taste and smell of that to help me relax and eliminate the distractions awaiting me. Other people I know prefer a scented candle to remind them that they are the light of the world. The key is to find what works for you and helps you to nurture your relationship with Jesus. Some people are more sensory and others are more cognitive. The key is to get a good mix of all the things we've talked about in this book—not every day, but definitely throughout the week and month.

However you start and whatever you do, keep in mind that your morning devotional time has three major elements: praise/worship, prayer, and Scripture. I heard recently that praise is one of the things that is missing most in the lives of believers today. It is wonderful to begin the day singing to our Lord and praising Him for his love, mercy, and grace. Praise is different than thanksgiving in that it is not thanking God for things He has done—it is praising Him for who He is. Try doing an Internet search for God's attributes and see what you come up with. Praise is important because it reminds you of whom God is, how much you need Him in your life, and how much He really has to offer.

After praise I usually like to talk to God next. You can find countless good books and Web sites on prayer out there so we won't get into a lot of detail here, but one of the best formats I know of is the ACTS acronym. A is for adoration and ties right in with praising God, as we've just discussed; C is for confession and helps us to give up our burdens to God and have a lighter load to carry through the day; T is for thanksgiving, which thanks God for specific things He has done for you in your life and offers a great time to look for and appreciate the miracles He has been working in it; finally, S is for supplication. Supplications are your requests, the things you need help with and the desires of your heart. And remember that praying for peace in your heart is a lot more likely to be granted than a new car. Beware of praying for patience, because that may bring on some situations in which you really have to grit your teeth and learn it the hard way! God is not some cosmic Santa Claus just dropping gifts in your lap. We really only learn and grow as Christians through trials and hard work—that's why we pray for peace in the midst of it all.

Finally, we must not forget Scripture. If all you do during your devotional time is sit quietly sipping tea and talking, you may end up finding that you've been speaking only to yourself and eventually realize that you're more New Age than Christian! Beware of anyone that tells you to empty your mind, because when you do that, you never know what will end up filling it. The goal of Christian devotions is not to clean out your mind but to fill it with God and His Word. Scripture is a vital part of being Christian and having a relationship with God. It is absolutely indispensible! Only through Scripture can we learn to hear the voice of God and understand His ways.

This book has been saturated with Scripture, because without it we will never come to a true knowledge of God and enter into a meaningful relationship with Him. Scripture purifies our relationship with God as we learn to know Him as He really is and not just how we want Him to be. Refer back to the earlier chapters in this book to remind yourself how to interact with Scripture. The insights I shared from Psalms 18, 23, and 63 all came from praying those passages again and again three to five times per week for months and sometimes even years. Most people have learned to read Scripture quickly and get a brief overview. But here the goal is to go deep and really think about the meaning, and then remember that you are not finished until you apply it to your life. If Scripture isn't changing the way you live, then you are not engaging it properly!

MIDDAY: CHECK-IN TIME. The morning devotional time may sound complex, but once you get going it is really very easy and rewarding—it's your foundation for the day. Now at midday, take just 10 to 15 minutes to mentally review your morning devotional time and lock it into your mind. Think of ways that you could have applied what you have learned throughout the morning and whom you may be able to share it with in the afternoon. The key here is to keep in mind that God is at your side no matter how good or bad your day is going. He is with you everywhere that you go. It is a reminder to talk to Him and remember His words in all that you say and do.

EVENING: REFLECTING ON YOUR DAY. At the end of the day it is time to sit back and relax with your Savior. Do you know that watching TV or surfing the Internet actually takes energy while spending time with God relieves stress and brings peace that eventually gives you more energy for the next day? I'm not saying never watch TV or surf the 'Net—just that only doing those things and leaving God out is rather destructive.

Research suggests that stress causes most of the physical ailments in our world today. Many people try to relieve the day's stress in the evening with alcohol, drugs, overeating, entertainment, and a whole host of other things, but only Jesus gives the true peace that people are looking for.

Sitting down for a few minutes before going to bed and thinking about your morning devotions further locks them into your mind. Evaluating how you handled stressful situations throughout the day and what you wish you would have done better can give you hope for an improved tomorrow. Praising God can bring you great joy and peace. And praying for Him to fill your life and lead you in specific ways can be life-changing. Now is also a great time to pray for family and friends and for God to use you in the lives of others. Beginning the day with God, taking time for Him throughout your day, and ending the day with Him helps make for a restful night's sleep and a better tomorrow.

Chapters 22-25

The Personal Practice of Living Devotionally: A Four-Week Daily Guide

In the next four chapters the devotional guides will incorporate scriptures that we have already studied in this book, allowing you to refer back to some of the insights that we shared so that there will be no risk of running out of material to think and pray about and to apply to your life. I will also include a few Ellen G. White quotes with the same themes along with suggestions for topics to pray about.

We will repeat some passages of Scripture each day of the week so that you have a chance to really understand them. One of the greatest injustices we do to Scripture is to gloss over it through a cursory reading. When you study a passage for several days, it sinks into your mind as you memorize it. Only then will it begin to help guide your life. Also, feel free to include some of the sights, sounds, smells, and tastes of the Old Testament sanctuary that we discussed earlier if it makes for a richer experience for you.

As you progress through this four-week devotional guide, keep track of what you relate to best. Record which books of the Bible and which times of day are most effective for you personally. This will help you to be the most successful as you begin to set up your own personal devotional life in chapter 26.

On the weekends we have included only one set of activities that you can engage in any time you like during each day. Monday through Friday we have broken each day into three activities that fit into a typical workday routine. Once you have completed this four-week exercise, you can then set up your own routine that you have found works best for you.

Chapter 22

The Personal Practice of Living Devotionally: Week 1

Sabbath

Think back over your experience at church this morning. What did you learn from Sabbath school, song service, prayer, offering, fellowship, and the sermon? What can you apply to your devotional life (10 minutes)?

Review chapter 14 (on Psalm 23) so that the details of the passage will be fresh in your mind for the week (20-25 minutes).

Spend some time talking to God about your hopes and concerns regarding this devotional journey you are embarking on (5-10 minutes).

Sunday

Bring to mind every memory verse you can remember from your childhood. Write them all down and begin considering ways in which you can apply them to your life throughout each day this week (30 minutes).

Thank God for all the scriptures you learned as a child even though you may not have understood why it was important at the time (5 minutes).

Monday

☑ **MORNING:** Review your best memories of church and of Jesus as you grew up and thank God for them (3-5 minutes). Recite as many memory verses from your childhood as you can remember (5-15 minutes). Take some time to reflect on the following passage (10-20 minutes):

⇧ "The Lord is my shepherd; I shall not want. He maketh me to lie down in green pastures: he leadeth me beside still waters He restoreth my soul: he leadeth me in the paths of righteousness for his name's sake. Yea, though I walk through the valley of the shadow of death, I will fear no evil: for thou art with me; thy rod and thy staff they comfort me. Thou preparest a table before me in the presence of mine enemies: thou anointest my head with oil; my cup runneth over. Surely goodness and mercy shall follow me all the days of my life: and I will dwell in the house of the Lord for ever" (Ps. 23, KJV).

☑ **MIDDAY:** Try reciting Psalm 23 from memory. Which part stands out to you just now (5-10 minutes)? Thank God for the spiritual foundation laid in your life as a child (3-5 minutes).

☑ **EVENING:** Think about these questions (10 minutes): Did you choose Jesus as your shepherd this morning? Did your actions today prove that you did? Think of the last time that you either symbolically or even literally laid down in green pastures. How did it feel? What does it mean for Jesus to restore your soul?

⇧ Talk to Jesus and allow Him to restore your soul as you go to sleep tonight (10-20 minutes).

Tuesday

☑ **MORNING:** Praise God for being your shepherd and comforter. Try to think specifically of everything He does for you in those roles (3-5 minutes). Consider the following passage and questions (10-15 minutes):

⇧ "The shepherd who discovers that one of his sheep is missing does not look carelessly upon the flock that is safely housed, and say, "I have ninety and nine, and it will cost me too much trouble to go in search of the straying one. Let him come back, and I will open the door of the sheepfold, and let him in." No; no sooner does the sheep go astray than the shepherd is filled with grief and anxiety. He counts and recounts the flock. When he is sure that one sheep is lost, he slumbers not. He leaves the ninety and nine within the fold, and goes in search of the straying sheep. The darker and more tempestuous the night and the more perilous the way, the greater is the shepherd's anxiety and the more earnest his search. He makes every effort to find that one lost sheep" (*Christ's Object Lessons*, pp. 187, 188).

⇧ Have you ever been a lost sheep? When? Have you ever thanked Jesus for searching for you and bringing you back? Pray for any lost sheep you might think of right now. Pray and ask the Lord to be your Shepherd today (3-5 minutes). Listen to your favorite Christian song (4-6 minutes).

☑ **MIDDAY:** Try reciting Psalm 23 from memory. Which part stands out to you just now (5-10 minutes)? Pray and thank God for the promise that "you shall not want." Thank God for providing for your necessities (3-5 minutes). This afternoon, find out how many of your friends at work or school know Psalm 23.

☑ **EVENING:** Spend some time in silent reflection on your day and explore the following questions (5-10 minutes):

⇧ Did you allow God to lead you into paths of righteousness today?

⇧ Where did you see God at work around you today? How did people respond when you asked them about Psalm 23?

⇧ Read Psalm 23 in your Bible and underline/highlight/write notes as you feel impressed (15-20 minutes). Go to sleep asking God where He wants to work in your life (10-15 minutes).

Wednesday

☑ **MORNING:** Listen to your favorite praise song (4-6 minutes). Pray for all your family members one by one (10-15 minutes). Pray through Psalm 23 (5-10 minutes).

☑ **MIDDAY:** Eat lunch alone with God today, either outside or looking out a window at some of His creation. Tell Him about your morning and ask Him about His day (10-15 minutes).

☑ **EVENING:** Spend some time in silent reflection on your day and dwell on the following questions (10-15 minutes):

⇧ Did you enjoy your lunchtime with God? What has been your favorite devotional time so far this week? Do you feel as though you are drawing closer to God? How is drawing closer to God affecting your other relationships?

⇧ Listen to the song "Draw Me Close," by Michael W. Smith (YouTube works well). Write a letter to God telling Him how you feel about the preceding questions. Ask Him to help you grow closer to Him every day.

Thursday

☑ **MORNING:** Light a candle and study its flame as you consider how God wants you to be the light of the world (3-5 minutes). Pray for everyone you know at work or school by name and ask God to show you whom He wants you to be a witness to (5-10 minutes). Reflect on the following passage (5-10 minutes):

⇧ "You are the salt of the earth. But what good is salt if it has lost its flavor? Can you make it salty again? It will be thrown out and trampled underfoot as worthless. You are the light of the world— like a city on a hilltop that cannot be hidden. No one lights a lamp and then puts it under a basket! Instead, a lamp is placed on a stand, where it gives light to everyone in the house. In the same way, let your good deeds shine out for all to see, so that everyone will praise your heavenly Father" (Matt. 5:13-16).

⇧ Pray for God's strength and power to be the light shining out of you today and for Him to give you the opportunity to encourage someone (3-5 minutes).

☑ **MIDDAY:** Think about whom you felt impressed to be a witness to this morning and how it went. Ask God to help you be even more successful this afternoon (5-10 minutes). Pray for some people that you do not know very well at work or school (3-5 minutes).

☑ **EVENING:** Take some time to reflect on your day and the paths of righteousness that God led you down. What went well? What would you like to go better tomorrow (10-15 minutes)? Has God been with you through any valleys of the shadow of death this week? How did He help you (3-5 minutes)? How do you feel about the fact that God wants to anoint you as His child and give you a good life (3-5 minutes)? Read the chapter in this book on Psalm 23 again to see if you can find more applications of its meaning in your life this past week (15-20 minutes). Talk to God as you would to a friend (5-10 minutes).

Friday

☑ **MORNING:** Read Psalm 63 in your favorite Bible and reflect on it (15-20 minutes). Praise God for your relationship with Him and ask it to grow. Ask Him to fill you with more love for Him. Then ask Him to fill you with more love for the people around you (5-10 minutes).

☑ **MIDDAY:** Think about the things you love most about God (3-5 minutes). Try to remember the theme of Psalm 63 that you read this morning (3-5 minutes). Smile at everyone you meet this afternoon and compliment those you know about something.

☑ **EVENING:** Read and reflect on chapter 3 (on Psalm 63) (15-20 minutes). Write one or two pages in your journal about your devotional experiences this past week (15-20 minutes). Tell God where you want your relationship with Him to go (5-10 minutes).

Chapter 23

The Personal Practice of Living Devotionally: Week 2

Sabbath

Review your experience at church this morning. What did you learn from Sabbath school, song service, prayer, offering, fellowship, and the sermon? What can you apply to your devotional life (10 minutes)? Read Ephesians 3:14-20 and the chapter in this book on it in preparation for this week's devotions (20-25 minutes). Pray the ACTS (adoration/confession/thanksgiving/supplication) prayer (5-10 minutes).

Sunday

Read the quote below and then try doing what it suggests. Open to your favorite Gospel for a reminder of the major events of Jesus' life or just think through everything that you can remember about His last few days before He died (1 hour):

"It would be well to spend a thoughtful hour each day reviewing the life of Christ from the manger to Calvary. We should take it point by point and let the imagination vividly grasp each scene, especially the closing ones of His earthly life. By thus contemplating His teachings and sufferings, and the infinite sacrifice made by Him for the redemption of the race, we may strengthen our faith, quicken our love, and become more deeply imbued with the spirit which sustained our Savior" (*Maranatha*, p. 77).

⇧ Spend some time talking to God about whatever is on your mind (5-10 minutes).

Monday

☑ **MORNING:** Try lighting some incense or a scented candle today. Sing or play your favorite hymn or praise song (3-5 minutes). Praise God for being your Creator. Think of how well He knows every bone in your body and every pain you've endured (3-5 minutes). Take some time to think about Jesus' birth and consider the following questions as they relate to the quote we looked at on Sunday. (10-15 minutes):

⇧ Why do you think the Creator volunteered to become the creature? How do you think God the Father felt as He watched from heaven? Why do you think the wise men brought incense? Why do you think incense was considered to be so valuable? Why do you think God instructed the priests to burn incense in the sanctuary? How do you feel when you burn incense during your devotional times?

⇧ Take some time to think about this passage (4-5 minutes):

⇧ "And may you have the power to understand, as all God's people should, how wide, how long, how high, and how deep his love is. May you experience the love of Christ, though it is too great to understand fully. Then you will be made complete with all the fullness of life and power that comes from God" (Eph. 3:18, 19).

⇧ ACTS prayer: adoration, confession, thanksgiving, supplication (3-5 minutes). Thank Him for loving you, and then quietly listen for His "still small voice" (3-5 minutes).

☑ **MIDDAY:** Remember and review in your mind Ephesians 3:18, 19 (3-5 minutes). Thank God for helping you get through the morning and ask Him to guide you through the rest of your day (2-3 minutes). Take some quiet time to think about what Jesus means to you (2-3 minutes).

☑ **EVENING:** Reflect on the following questions (10-15 minutes). Think through your day—how did it go? Where did you see God today? Pray and ask Him to show you the places where He was but you didn't notice. What would you like to do better with your devotional times tomorrow?

⇧ Review Ephesians 3:18, 19 again (3-5 minutes). Review the quote from *Maranatha* as you lay in bed and go to sleep (10-20 minutes).

Tuesday

☑ **MORNING:** Play one of your favorite praise songs (5-6 minutes). Pray for every friend and relative you can think of for the next 10 minutes. Tell God your favorite memory of growing up (3-5 minutes). Read through Ephesians 3:14-20 and reflect on its meaning (10-15 minutes).

☑ **MIDDAY:** Sit quietly with God. Don't say a word—just enjoy His presence (5 minutes).

⇧ Think about the ways you can feel God's love in your life today (3-5 minutes). Call a friend or family member and ask them what they like best about God. Tell them what you like best about Him (5 minutes).

☑ **EVENING:** Think back through your day and identify both your victories and the things you wish that you'd done better. Was it hard to call someone and ask them what they like best about God (5-10 minutes)? Tell God about your worst nightmare (3-5 minutes). Imagine being immersed in God's love that is so wide, high, long, and deep (3-5 minutes). Write a letter to Him (10-15 minutes). Go to sleep thinking of ways that you can show His love to others (10-15 minutes).

Wednesday

☑ **MORNING:** Listen to three or four of your favorite worship songs (15-20 minutes). Sit quietly and listen for God's voice (5-10 minutes). Pray and ask God to be your shepherd today (3-5 minutes).

☑ **MIDDAY:** Read 1 Corinthians 13 and reflect on it (5-10 minutes). Ask God to help you show such love to the people around you this afternoon (3-5 minutes).

☑ **EVENING:** Read Ephesians 3:14-20 and then 1 Corinthians 13. How do they go together (15-20 minutes)? Write a prayer about God's love and what it means to you in your journal (10-15 minutes).

Thursday

☑ **MORNING:** Make your favorite hot drink to enjoy during your devotional time today.

⇧ Study 1 Corinthians 13 again. Is it a definition or description of God's love (10-15 minutes)?

⇧ Read John 3:16, 17 and reflect on it (3-5 minutes). Pray the ACTS prayer (5-10 minutes)

☑ **MIDDAY:** Sit in your car and listen to praise music while you worship God and talk to Him (10-15 minutes).

☑ **EVENING:** Walk around your neighborhood and tell the people you see that you are taking prayer requests and ask if they would like you to pray for something for them (20-30 minutes). As you lie in bed, pray for the people you met or saw this evening and ask God to show them His love in their lives (10-15 minutes).

Friday

☑ **MORNING:** Light a scented candle and make yourself a hot drink. Turn on some instrumental worship music and ask God to give you His power to be the light of the world as you look at the candle and reflect (15-20 minutes). Write in your journal about how God's love has empowered you this week (10-15 minutes).

☑ **MIDDAY:** Think about the Sabbath that is coming and consider how it is a love gift from God. Imagine how you want to spend time with Him this Sabbath (10-15 minutes).

☑ **EVENING:** Pray and thank God for the Sabbath rest (3-5 minutes). Sit silently in God's presence (3-5 minutes). Reflect on your outreach activities for the past two weeks. Was it easier to witness to coworkers, family, or the neighbors you passed on the sidewalk? (5-10 minutes). Which was most rewarding? Why? Review all the texts we read about love this week (15-20 minutes). Ask God to help you experience His love every day and let it shine out of you into all the world (3-5 minutes).

Chapter 24

The Personal Practice
of Living Devotionally: Week 3

Sabbath

Tell one or more of your friends today about the devotional journey you've been on and what it means to you (20-30 minutes). Review the chapter on Psalm 18 in preparation for this week's devotional times (20-30 minutes). Pray for God to reveal His power to you this week (3-5 minutes).

Sunday

Study Ezekiel 1 (20-30 minutes). Pray to God in adoration of whom He is. Thank Him for the privilege of talking to the king of the universe (3-5 minutes).

Monday

☑ **MORNING:** Light a scented candle and prepare your favorite hot drink. Listen to the song "Awesome God," by Brent Miller or another Christian artist (5-10 minutes). Read Exodus 19:16-20 and reflect on God's power (5-10 minutes). Pray the ACTS prayer, spending extra time on adoration (5-10 minutes). Listen to "Awesome God" again (5 minutes).

☑ **MIDDAY:** Get out in nature and spend time in silence and prayer, listening for God's still small voice (10-15 minutes).

☑ **EVENING:** Pray to Jesus thanking Him for being a God of power and love. Ask Him to help you understand how power and gentleness go together (5-10 minutes). Read Exodus 20:18-21 and the pages in this book that comment on it (15-20 minutes). Spend some time journaling how you feel about God's power and His tender love. Do you think you are more like the Israelites who were afraid of God or like Moses who couldn't wait to be with Him? Why? (10-15 minutes).

Tuesday

☑ **MORNING:** Read Revelation 4 three or four times and reflect on it (15-20 minutes).

⇧ Listen to the "Revelation Song," as recorded by Kari Jobe (10-15 minutes). Think about what it will be like to be in God's presence and worshipping Him in heaven (3-5 minutes).

☑ **MIDDAY:** Pray for God to help you grasp the concept of a loving God that has amazing and unlimited power. Reflect on what that means for your life (10-15 minutes). Tell someone about God's awesome power and His tender love.

☑ **EVENING:** Read Revelation 18 and reflect on it. Spend some time journaling how you feel about God's power (15-20 minutes). As you lie in bed, think about the fact that God is infinitely more powerful than the devil. Now, talk to your God, the most powerful and loving force in the universe, about everything that happened to you today. Take comfort in His presence (15-20 minutes).

Wednesday

☑ **MORNING:** Read Psalm 104:1-13 and try to picture what it must have looked like when God created the world (15-20 minutes). Listen to "Awesome God" (5-10 minutes). Pray for your loved ones by name—especially that they may feel God's presence in their lives (5-10 minutes).

☑ **MIDDAY:** Listen to your favorite praise songs that tell of God's power (10-15 minutes).

⇧ Tell God how much you love Him (3-5 minutes).

☑ **EVENING:** Light a candle and make yourself a hot drink. Go somewhere quiet and listen for the voice of God (15 minutes). Now tell Him everything that is on your mind with full knowledge that He is listening (15-20 minutes).

Thursday

☑ **MORNING:** Write a two-page essay in your journal entitled "What

I Would Like God to Do With His Power." How do you think God would feel about what you wrote? (20-30 minutes).

⇧ Reflect on how you use the power that He has entrusted to you. Ask Him to help you use your strength and influence wisely (5-10 minutes).

☑ **MIDDAY:** Rest quietly in God's presence. Close your eyes and don't say a word (10-15 minutes).

☑ **EVENING:** Send an e-mail to your best friends telling them about your devotional journey and how it's shaping your view of God (15-20 minutes). Pray the ACTS prayer (3-5 minutes).

Friday
☑ **MORNING:** Listen to the "Revelation Song" (6-12 minutes).

⇧ Read Revelation 4 and reflect on it (5-10 minutes). Listen to "Awesome God" (5-10 minutes).

☑ **MIDDAY:** Call someone you love and tell them how much they mean to you (5-10 minutes). Thank God for the people in your life who love you. Thank God for each of them by name (3-5 minutes).

☑ **EVENING:** Review and reflect on all the scriptures that we've looked at this week (30-45 minutes). Read John 3:16, 17. Pray and tell God how you feel about the fact that He wants to use His power to save you rather than condemn you. Remind yourself that Jesus would have died for you—even if you were the only one (5-10 minutes).

Chapter 25

The Personal Practice of Living Devotionally: Week 4

Sabbath

Tell your pastor about the devotional journey you're on and how it's influencing your life (5-10 minutes). Think back over your experience at church this morning. What did you learn from Sabbath school, song service, prayer, offering, fellowship, and the sermon? What can you apply to your devotional life (10 minutes)? Read Exodus 20, then review chapter 12 (on the first four of the Ten Commandments) (30-45 minutes).

Sunday

Throughout the day, memorize the order of the Ten Commandments (don't worry about all the details of the fourth). Pray the ACTS prayer (10-15 minutes).

Monday

☑ **MORNING:** Pray through the first four commandments, applying them to your life and intentionally choosing to follow God today (15-20 minutes). Praise God for His strength and power, then for His love and goodness. Thank God for giving you the Ten Commandments as a guide for your life (5-10 minutes). Sit in silence, listening for the voice of God (5-10 minutes).

☑ **MIDDAY:** Listen to some worship music and talk to God (10-15 minutes).

☑ **EVENING:** Read over the following quote and then try doing what it suggests. Open to your favorite Gospel for a reminder of the major events of Jesus life or just think through everything you can remember about His last few days before His death (1 hour).

⇧ "It would be well to spend a thoughtful hour each day reviewing the life of Christ from the manger to Calvary. We should take it point by point and let the imagination vividly grasp each scene, especially the closing ones of His earthly life. By thus contemplating His teachings and sufferings, and the infinite sacrifice made by Him for the redemption of the race, we may strengthen our faith, quicken our love, and become more deeply imbued with the spirit which sustained our Savior" (*Maranatha,* p. 77).

⇧ Spend some time talking to God about whatever is on your mind (5-10 minutes).

Tuesday

☑ **MORNING:** Think about Moses meeting with God personally on Mount Sinai. If you could speak to God in person, what would you talk about? (5-10 minutes). Pray the ACTS prayer (5-10 minutes). Listen to worship music while you drive to school or work (15-20 minutes).

☑ **MIDDAY:** Text a friend to tell them that you are praying for them. Ask if they have any requests (3-5 minutes). Forget about whatever has been going on all day and relax in God's presence (5-10 minutes).

☑ **EVENING:** Light a candle and sit down with a glass of cold grape juice and some wheat crackers. Think about the blood that Jesus shed for you and look at the grape juice and crackers as a symbol of His sacrifice (3-5 minutes). Read 1 Corinthians 11:23-29 and reflect on it (10-15 minutes). Write in your journal about Jesus' sacrifice and how it relates to the first four commandments (15-20 minutes).

Wednesday

☑ **MORNING:** Read 1 Thessalonians 5:16-18 and reflect on it. Ask God to help you memorize the passage (5-10 minutes). Try to think about God and talk to Him for at least one minute every hour today. Set a reminder alarm in your clock or computer. Start now (1 minute). Pray the ACTS prayer while you drive to school or work (15-20 minutes).

☑ **MIDDAY:** Have you successfully talked to God for at least one minute each hour today? Thank God for your success and ask Him to help you do better. Consider what impact thinking of God more frequently is having on you and how you believe it will affect you as you get better at it (10-15 minutes).

☑ **EVENING:** Light a candle and study its flame as you pray and ask God to shine out through you as the light of the world. Ask Him how He wants you to shine (10-15 minutes). Read Exodus 20 and then read chapter 13 (on the last six of the Ten Commandments). Reflect on what it means to "love your neighbor as yourself" (30-40 minutes).

Thursday

☑ **MORNING:** Review the last six of the Ten Commandments in your mind (you have memorized them now) and make plans for how you can live them out today (10-15 minutes).

⇧ Try to think about God and talk to Him for at least one minute every hour today. Set a reminder alarm in your clock or computer. Talk to God while you drive to work or school or take a walk (10-15 minutes).

☑ **MIDDAY:** Find a "neighbor" to show God's love to during lunch. Look around you and ask God to direct you to the person who needs Him. Pray for God to give you the words to say as you reach out (10-15 minutes).

☑ **EVENING:** Call or write to your parents or other close relatives and tell them that you love them (10-15 minutes).

⇧ Practice "loving your neighbor as yourself" by calling or writing to the people you have wronged recently, tell them about the devotional journey you are on, and ask for their forgiveness (15-20 minutes).

Friday

☑ **MORNING:** Listen to your favorite worship songs as you reflect on your devotional journey of the past few weeks (10-15 minutes). Try to think about God and talk to Him for at least one minute every hour today. Set a reminder alarm in your clock or computer. Sing and/or speak praises to God as you drive to work or school (10-15 minutes).

☑ **MIDDAY:** Tell God how much you love Him and why (3-5 minutes). Think through your favorite scriptures that you have memorized (5-10 minutes).

☑ **EVENING:** Take some time to reflect and journal on your devotional journey of the past few weeks. Review your journaling, highlighting, and notes (30-45 minutes). Pray and ask God whom He wants you to share these experiences with. Pray and ask God for the names of three to five people that you can start a small group with, inviting them to embrace a personal devotional journey as well (10-15 minutes). Now "go ye therefore into all the world making disciples" (the rest of your life).

Chapter 26

Setting Up Your Personal Daily Devotional Routine

I hope that you're finding the devotional journey to be an exciting one! It takes commitment and discipline, but the rewards are more than worth the effort as you feel peace, confidence, and purpose filling your life. Now it's time to take the next step and develop your own customized devotional routine. It may sound like a daunting task, but I assure you that you can do it with God's help and a few basic principles. Remember to refer back to chapter 21 for the structural overview of the devotional life and then check out the rest of this chapter for some helpful suggestions on the content to put into that structure. Once you get it going, you'll see that it's really quite simple.

Now that you've had four weeks to try out a variety of devotional tools, I'm sure you've found that you like some better than others. People that gravitate to deeper Bible study may not be as interested in the more sensory elements such as incense or representations of the candelabra, and those more attracted to Christian music may have less interest in Bible study. But the bottom line is that you need to have a healthy and well-balanced spiritual diet. Here are the basic categories of devotional elements that I used in structuring the past four weeks. You should be sure to include all of them to some degree as you set up your own devotional routine.

Cognitive Nourishment

☑ **SCRIPTURE:** Reading from the Bible or using memorized scriptures

☑ **PRAYER:** Can include all of the ACTS (adoration, confession, thanksgiving, supplication) elements or focus on one at a time

☑ **REFLECTION:** Taking time to think about and apply a passage to your life

Emotional Nourishment

☑ **WORSHIP:** Singing and/or listening to Christian music or watching praise music videos on YouTube

☑ **SENSORY:** Including some of the sanctuary symbols such as incense, a candelabra (or a simple scented candle), showbread (or other taste elements such as a hot drink) in your devotional times

☑ **JOURNALING:** Writing down your thoughts and reflections on Scripture and the Christian life

Exercise

☑ **OUTREACH:** Helping others in various ways, including encouragement/support and sharing spiritual thoughts, scriptures, and testimonies

⇧ I personally engage Scripture, prayer, and reflection every day (not necessarily all three during each devotional time) and outreach in some form almost every day. As for journaling, worship, and sensory experiences, I alternate them as I feel the need (I will typically include one of them each day—occasionally two). This is a sample outline of the elements I included in the first week's Monday through Friday devotional routine in chapter 21:

Monday

☑ **MORNING:** Reflection/Scripture/prayer

☑ **MIDDAY:** Reflection/Scripture/prayer

☑ **EVENING:** Reflection/prayer

Tuesday

☑ **MORNING:** Prayer/reflection/worship

☑ **MIDDAY:** Scripture/reflection/prayer/outreach

☑ **EVENING:** Reflection/Scripture/journaling/prayer

Wednesday
☑ **MORNING:** Worship/prayer/Scripture

☑ **MIDDAY:** Reflection/prayer

☑ **EVENING:** Reflection/worship/journaling/prayer

Thursday
☑ **MORNING:** Sensory experience/reflection/Scripture/prayer/outreach

☑ **MIDDAY:** Reflection/prayer

☑ **EVENING:** Reflection/Scripture/prayer

Friday
☑ **MORNING:** Scripture/prayer/reflection

☑ **MIDDAY:** Reflection/outreach

☑ **EVENING:** Reflection/Scripture/journaling/prayer

Some of you will want to outline your devotions for the week as you set them up each Sabbath, and others of you won't want to be so formal. The point is to think about the devotional elements you include in your routine and make sure that you maintain a healthy balance. In the past the tendency for many people has been to emphasize only Bible or devotional book reading along with prayer, which led to very little reflection and application of biblical principles, little to no outreach, and little to no emotional attachment to God. It is clearly evident in David's Psalm 93 that he was very emotionally attached to God, the reason that the Bible calls him "a man after God's own heart." The goal of devotional time is more than head knowledge—it's to have a well-balanced and healthy relationship with Jesus.

When you consider Christ's life on earth, ask yourself what was the difference between the crowds that followed Him so adoringly and the disciples? Both groups enjoyed listening to Jesus' teachings, many spent time talking with Him, and both groups wanted Him to become king. But one of the main differences between the two categories was that the crowds wanted Jesus to make "them" comfortable by receiving food and healing from Him. They were in it for what they could get for themselves, and when they didn't get all they wanted, they ended up turning on Him and shouting, "Crucify Him!"

Jesus' disciples, on the other hand, eventually got to the point where their love for Him grew so great that they wanted to be partners with Him in ministry. Eventually they all died serving Him—most as martyrs. An intimate and emotional attachment nurtured in a personal relationship with Jesus naturally leads to outreach and devotion/emotional attachment. Thus both elements must have a place in your devotional life.

Finding Devotional Passages of Scripture

In setting up a devotional life I have found that most people have some favorite Christian songs that they enjoy—any genre will do as long as you relate to it personally. Even though many people grow up thinking of prayer primarily as a time to ask God for things, they can easily understand the importance of adoration, confession, and thanksgiving once presented with it. And most people also quickly understand the importance of reflection and journaling—if you don't think things through, you can't internalize and live them. When it comes to the more sensory elements of worship, some people grasp them and embrace them as though they've just found the final piece of the puzzle that they didn't know was missing, while others more cognitive in nature may view such sensory elements with suspicion. But we are all different and have varying needs, and since every devotional element discussed here is clearly biblical, it is important to embrace them all on one level or another.

It is interesting to note, however, that the most difficult devotional element for people to fully grasp and incorporate into their lives is Scripture. Most people feel convicted that the Bible is by far the most important devotional element, but the problem is that they struggle to know where to turn in Scripture to find the nourishment they are looking for. Reading the Bible from cover to cover in a year isn't necessarily a devotional approach—it gives you an overview of Scripture, but it doesn't give you specifically what you need to help you deal with what you are facing on a particular day. It is imperative that you understand where to go in the Bible in order to find what you need at a particular time. Here we will look at a simple overview of the Bible to help you figure out where to look so that you can get what you need to help you through your day.

Old Testament
☑ **PENTATEUCH (BOOKS OF MOSES)**
⇧ Genesis-Deuteronomy

☑ **HISTORY BOOKS**
⇧ Joshua-Esther

☑ **PSALMS AND POETRY**
⇧ Job-Song of Solomon

☑ **PROPHETS (MAJOR AND MINOR)**
⇧ Isaiah-Zechariah

New Testament
☑ **GOSPELS**
⇧ Matthew-John

☑ **HISTORY**
⇧ Acts of the Apostles

☑ **PAUL'S LETTERS**
⇧ Romans-Philemon

☑ **GENERAL LETTERS AND REVELATION**
⇧ Hebrews-Revelation

Traditionally, Psalms and the Gospels are the "go to" books for devotions. Psalms is the most emotional—with all of David's crying out in joy and despair—and in the Gospels you can follow the life and teachings of Jesus, seeing how to live and how to involve yourself in Christian outreach. But some days you may feel a need for more instruction or teachings to clarify your walk with God. When that happens, look through the New Testament letters. The apostles specifically wrote them to help people understand the gospel teachings better and apply them to their lives. Galatians and Ephesians are classic favorites here, and those more cognitive in nature prize the book of Romans. Should you desire inspiring miracle stories, check out Exodus, some of the historical battles in Judges, and the historical book of Acts when the church was just getting started. The most colorful love letter in the Bible is of course Song of Solomon. If you love prophecies that can be more devotional in nature, check out Isaiah and Ezekiel. Some people can read Daniel and Revelation in a devotional way—but for most people those are "study" books. Then as you look over a book whose topic interests you, browse through the headings that mark off passages within each chapter to narrow your search down. Here are a few of my favorite passages that you can choose from to help get you started:

⇧ Deuteronomy 32:1-4

⇧ Psalm 104

⇧ John 14:1-3

⇧ Hebrews 12:1-3

⇧ Matthew 6:5-15

⇧ Psalm 51

⇧ Isaiah 53

⇧ Jeremiah 29:11-13

⇧ Hosea 1

That should help you at least to get a start. Spend some free time simply browsing Scripture, looking for devotional passages. As you do, develop a collection of your favorites for future use. Talk to friends who are on the devotional journey as well, and share your testimonies of what's working for you and what's not and why. The devotional journey is a shared one when it's at its best. So dig in, pray for the Holy Spirit to guide you, invite some friends to join you, review the structure and principles outlined here, and go for it. Live your life with Jesus the best you know how, and He will bless you beyond your wildest dreams.

Chapter 27

Living the Life!

Hear, O Israel! The Lord is our God, the Lord alone. And you must love the Lord your God with all your heart, all your soul, and all your strength. And you must commit yourselves wholeheartedly to these commands that I am giving you today. Repeat them again and again to your children. Talk about them when you are at home and when you are on the road, when you are going to bed and when you are getting up. Tie them to your hands and wear them on your forehead as reminders. Write them on the doorposts of your house and on your gates" (Deut. 6:4-9).

This passage in Deuteronomy defines the goal of this book—to live your life with Jesus everywhere you go and in everything you do from the time you wake up in the morning till the time you go to bed at night. God wants to saturate your life with His Word and His Spirit and continual conversations with Jesus. Known as the Shema by the ancient Israelites, Deuteronomy 6:4-9 was the foundation of their lives.

Just as the Israelites of old gathered manna every day to sustain them physically as they wandered in the wilderness, so God now wants us to gather spiritual manna daily to sustain our devotional lives as we wander in the spiritual wilderness of our time. Yesterday's spiritual manna will not be good for tomorrow—we must nourish ourselves spiritually every day. The spiritual manna we gather every day is the passages of Scripture that we read, the prayers we offer, the time spent reflecting on God and life with Him, and our worship and journaling that gives us the strength to reach out to others as we partake in fulfilling the gospel commission while filled with the Spirit.

Ultimately, pursuing a life with Jesus will lead to an almost effortless comfort with Him and a sense of ease in His presence—just like an old married couple that still cherishes each other's company even after 50 years together. They learn to know each other's likes and dislikes and sense the other's thoughts before they speak them. The love and security you find in such a devotional life will be beyond what words can express. You will learn that true life springs forth from your devotional times with God. At times you may even find yourself staying up all night in prayer and communion with your heavenly Father during the hardest times of your life just as Jesus did. It will be the strength of that relationship that sees you through the darkest valleys that you will face.

It will also be this relationship that causes you to continue running back to God after you fall. Just as He did for Peter, Jesus will pull you back to your feet as you begin sinking into the waves because you took your eyes off Him. Jesus will lovingly restore you even if you deny Him three times in a row as Peter did when He needed the disciple the most. Always remember that no matter what you do, Jesus will always take you back into His loving arms and hold you. That's how families are—they take you back because you're one of them. Our Father in heaven is always forgiving even when others in the family may not be. Then, just as we know how we would always like to be accepted and restored after we make a mistake, we also need to forgive others and accept them back after they have fallen or sinned against us as well.

Then we have the privilege of inviting new people to join the family. It used to be that when we engaged in outreach evangelism, people wanted to see what we "believed" before they would agree to "belong." Many referred to it as "believing then belonging." Now, some suggest that people want to "belong then believe"—as in get to know us and then learn about and accept what we believe about God and the Bible. But I don't think that's the case at all. Rather, people today want us to stop making it all about beliefs and make it about Jesus.

We need to stop fighting over whose beliefs are better, and learn to love each other first. I believe it's 100 percent about belonging—period. Beliefs cannot stand alone. Making sense only in the context of a relationship with Jesus, beliefs purify and strengthen the relationship. But we must first invite people to belong to the church family—then belong to Jesus. That is to say, we start out by encouraging others to join the community of people who love Jesus—the ones who will show them the way to live with Him. Then, with the example and support of the Christian community, they will learn to give themselves to Jesus and belong to Him as well. It's all about belonging! The beliefs are critically important—they help you understand how you belong and why you belong—but it's still about belonging and relationships. This is relationship theology—it is what Jesus lived and how we should follow His example.

I think this is how my own spirituality got derailed. As a kid I loved church and everything about it—it was what our lives revolved around. Church, Sabbath school, Pathfinders, potlucks, church picnics, and socializing at other church members' homes—I loved it all. It was my world, and a good one at that. I felt a great sense of belonging in my church family. But when I hit my teens, it was time for me to start belonging to Jesus—but no one ever told me that or showed me it in a way I could understand. I received only beliefs, routines, and activities. The beliefs and activities, such as church attendance, abstinence, and morals, were good, but it seemed that they were to be an end in themselves rather than leading me to another end—that of knowing Jesus personally. So "belonging, then believing" didn't work for me, and it isn't working for many others like me, either.

Now I recognize that it's *all* about Jesus. It's about knowing and loving Him as a personal God, Savior, and Friend. It's about understanding Him for who He really is. And it's about learning His ways in His Word so that I know how to order my ways and live my life to the fullest too. This is why beliefs are important—they clarify our understanding of who God really is. Even more, it's also about experiencing God's power in my life—power to live beyond myself and my own capabilities by allowing Him to live in and work through me. And finally, it's about living life devotionally—walking and talking with Him every day.

Ultimately, it's simply about living life with Jesus, walking hand in hand with Him through the ups and the downs, the victories and defeats, the love and the shame—through all that life on earth has to offer. I know that He is here beside me to help me through it all one step at a time, one day at a time, from now until the end of my days. But that's the bonus, isn't it? When we choose Jesus, our days will never end permanently. Death may interrupt them for a time, but they will eventually go on through the ceaseless ages of eternity. So invite people into your home and to your small groups and into your lives. Invite them to "belong" in your life. Then invite them to "belong" to Jesus by making Him their best friend. Walk with them down this road together, strengthening and encouraging each other. As you make the journey with them, share beliefs by talking "about them when you are at home and when you are on the road, when you are going to bed and when you are getting up" (Deut. 11:19).

Belonging to the family, belonging to Jesus, and learning about Him along the way—it's beautiful in its simplicity. So if you don't have one, form a small group. Engage Scripture, prayer, reflection, worship, journaling, and outreach together and individually with your friends and with Jesus. Then enjoy simply living the life that Jesus has had planned for you from the beginning of time as you continue to reach out to others all along the way—never ceasing to share the joy that is within you. This, I believe, is the ultimate fulfillment of the great gospel commission.

"Christ's method alone will give true success in reaching the people. The Savior mingled with men as one who desired their good. He showed His sympathy for them, ministered to their needs, and won their confidence. Then He bade them, 'Follow Me'" (*The Ministry of Healing,* p. 143).